This Book Is for You If

- You want to enhance your relationship or marriage.

- You hope to heal from a painful breakup, divorce, or a partner's death.

- You want to set the course for a desired future relationship.

- You yearn to uncover and express your authentic self in your relationship.

- You want your marriage to keep pace with your ongoing personal growth.

- You strive to harmonize your marital well-being on physical, emotional, mental, and spiritual levels.

- You long to expand your heart's capacity to create and sustain your sacred relationship.

Secrets
OF A
SOULFUL
MARRIAGE

Creating
&
Sustaining a
Loving, Sacred Relationship

JIM SHARON, EdD, AND RUTH SHARON, MS

Walking Together, Finding the Way®

SKYLIGHT PATHS®
PUBLISHING
Woodstock, Vermont

Secrets of a Soulful Marriage:
Creating and Sustaining a Loving, Sacred Relationship

2014 Quality Paperback Edition, First Printing
© 2014 by Jim Sharon and Ruth Sharon

Library of Congress Cataloging-in-Publication Data
Available upon request.

10 9 8 7 6 5 4 3 2 1

Manufactured in the United States of America
Cover Design: Jenny Buono
Interior Design: Tim Holtz

Walking Together, Finding the Way
Published by SkyLight Paths Publishing
A Division of LongHill Partners, Inc.
Sunset Farm Offices, Route 4, P.O. Box 237
Woodstock, VT 05091
Tel: (802) 457-4000 Fax: (802) 457-4004
www.skylightpaths.com

Contents

Introduction

The message on an anniversary greeting card that we enjoyed receiving:

Current Marriage Trends—"Staying single is chic.
Divorce is in vogue. Living together is common.
And here YOU are, happily married.
Hmmm—kinky!"

Having been soulfully married since 1970, we are proud to be a kinky exception to the trends cited in that cute anniversary card.

Our purpose in writing this book is to enhance and enrich couples' relationships by sharing our personal experiences and those of other deeply committed spouses. Also, we want to offer useful perspectives, tools, and practices that we have acquired over forty years of experience as marriage counselors and, more recently, as coaches for soulful couples. We are passionate about fostering beautiful, sacred relationships. Moreover, we envision a powerful ripple effect emanating from love-filled marriages to the evolving consciousness of humanity.

Over the course of human history, the structure of a man and a woman living together has evolved from primarily being an effective means of survival to forging an emotional and spiritual bond. Prehistoric humans joined together as couples to procreate the human species and to meet basic needs in a cooperative hunter-gatherer society. Contemporary marriages have become multidimensional and much more complex than those in ancient times. In recent decades, the roles of men and women have become less well defined. For example, many men are homemakers or primary child-care providers and numerous women are corporate executives. Our ancestors' partnerships were purely based on survival. Our modern relationships offer the possibility to support our individual life pursuits, as well as our fulfillment as couples.

What Is a Soulful Marriage?

In a normal, healthy relationship, you may get along well with your partner in the practical aspects of life. What about expanding the spectrum of your experience to include sacred and spiritual aspects? Imagine the facets of a diamond engagement ring gleaming in the sunlight. You have the potential to make your relationship as brilliant and dazzling as a precious, polished diamond.

In a soulful relationship, you are dedicated to being true to yourself and to supporting your partner's overall well-being. You commit to doing personal growth work, expanding your ability to love yourself and your partner. You open yourself to your partner by being vulnerable, real, present, and proactive. You need not hide your blemishes and weaknesses. You work to accept who you are—learning to laugh at yourself can be freeing. You grow in awareness of who you are. You maintain your individuality as you join with your partner in the quest for mutual personal and spiritual evolution.

Soulful relationships are a haven for creativity, growth, exploration, and inner peace. You are a well-wisher and witness to each other's unfolding personal growth. Listening and speaking with love and respect are cornerstones of a healthy relationship.

Being together as a couple takes on even more dimensions when you share your visions and dreams with each other. Building the life you long for is profoundly fulfilling. When you are feeling good about yourself and your relationship, you handle the stresses of everyday routines and challenges with more balance and grace. Your life becomes more meaningful and purposeful.

Do you hunger for a spiritual connection that is personally nourishing for you and your partner? This book may whet your appetite for more!

Secrets of a Soulful Marriage, based on our Coaching for Soulful Couples program, is dedicated to sharing the ancient and current wisdom of transforming your ordinary partnership into an exquisite masterpiece. The power and beauty of your love has the potential to ripple out for generations to come.

Embarking on the Journey as a Soulful Couple

An ambitious intention of this book is to help you view your individual and couple life through the lens of your soul. Creating and sustaining a soulful marriage is an ongoing journey. Our key premise, our highest ideal for soulful couples, may be stated as follows: You are spiritual beings having human experiences on earth, each with your own purpose. You support each other to fulfill your individual and shared purposes.

Each of you holds the secrets of what really works in your relationship. Perhaps you have not thought about or expressed your secrets. In reading this book and participating in soulful couples activities, you are likely to tap into your dormant wisdom and gain the courage to unlock those secrets.

In the pages that follow, we reveal the secrets that have helped us to be more loving and powerful as individuals and as a couple. Interspersed throughout the book are vignettes from couples who share their experiences on a soulful marriage path. You are not alone. You can draw from the shared wisdom of other committed couples to enrich your relationship.

Our hope is that you use this book to better articulate the secrets of what works in your relationship and what you each long for in your marriage. How can you live as best friends, lovers, roommates, healthy partners, parents, and spiritual beloveds? Learning to become more soulful as a couple is a lifelong process.

In this book, we guide you to be realistic about what is involved in creating and sustaining a soulful relationship. In the opening chapter, "Getting Personal," we encourage you to learn more about yourself and commit to your own growth. Transforming yourself and evolving take courage, commitment, and compassion. Doing the individual grunt work is crucial for viable, healthy relationships. Identifying old wounds and releasing your fears allow you to experience love, passion, joy, and satisfaction as a couple.

As you probably realize, when you expand your perception and envision what is possible, your long-held resistances come to the surface—together with fears and warnings about proceeding on this unknown path of change. How can you heed your concerns about changing and still proceed into the uncharted territory of sacred relationship? We guide you to master this paradox!

The practical guidelines and tools in chapter 2, "Breaking Loose," help you identify the defensive, often primitive survival patterns that have brought you to this present moment. We know that to be available to truly love and be loved, you need to examine your past and address any unhealed hurts or traumas. Self-awareness and healing are integral to developing a sacred relationship. Bookmark chapter 2 to use as a toolkit whenever you feel stuck in old patterns.

Enhancing healthy communication with your partner is the hallmark of a long-lasting and satisfying relationship. Chapter 3, "Speaking and Listening in a Dance," focuses on identifying and overcoming blocks to effective communication and offers numerous skill-building tips for strengthening your marriage.

Honoring and adoring your spouse is the theme of chapter 4, "Respecting and Cherishing Your Beloved." Learn simple ways to touch your spouse's heart in your daily life and to spiritually elevate your love. We encourage you to acknowledge and accept your individual styles of giving and receiving love.

If you are hoping to reignite your passion for each other, you will enjoy chapter 5, "Light Your Fire and Bask in the Warmth." Don't we all want more quality time together, romance, and satisfying lovemaking? Sparking and sustaining intimacy are among the true joys of marriage!

In chapter 6, "The Power and Beauty of a Balanced Life," we illustrate the importance of honoring the you, me, and us in your relationship. We offer suggestions for finding the spiritual center of your life and for recognizing and honoring your inner nature. Taking time each day to clear your mind, relax your body, and restore your soul provides an antidote to the pressures of overwhelming busyness. You serve your family and all those you influence by slowing down and creating inner harmony, ease, and centeredness.

Vital attitudes and skills for soulful parenting (and grandparenting) are highlighted in chapter 7, "Sustaining Your Soulful Relationship While Parenting." With the indescribable joy of raising children come strains on your resources and time. We show you ways to support each other to maintain your soulful relationship amid effective parenting. You will learn how to bring your own inner peace into your daily relationship with your children so that you function as a soulful family.

In chapter 8, "Vision for the Future," we present evocative imagery that inspires you and your mate to further expand your love and to extend it beyond your family. As a soulful couple, you are invited to consider what legacy you can leave to your children, your community, and perhaps even to the world. You'll learn to evoke your essential nature and clarify your vision for your future.

We conclude with "The Promise of Love" to open your perception and your heart to what is possible. The reality of relationships is that the initial bubble of romance eventually bursts under the pressures of everyday life. But when you cultivate a soulful relationship through compassion, self-care, couple care, and communication, you find that what develops after the bubble has popped is a deeper, more intimate, enduring love.

We are delighted that you have agreed to take this journey with us to new dimensions of soulful marriage. Here is a backpack of supplies you'll need:

- a willing heart
- an open mind
- eagerness to learn
- discipline to practice new skills and attitudes
- patience to persevere through rough terrain
- this book as a map of the territory
- a sense of direction and purpose
- a moral and intuitive compass
- a calendar to structure times to do the personal and couple practices and to plan in-house and out-of-the-house dates and activities

- a journal to record progress and milestones along the way
- gratitude for taking the journey with your partner

Shifts in Consciousness

To illuminate your path to a soulful relationship, we clarify some aspects of the shifts in consciousness that many of you may experience along the way. We describe prominent shifts in beliefs about relationships—from the conventional model to the evolving soulful model. These shifts often reflect changing cultural norms or debunk myths about what romantic partnership is or should be.

Personal Practice and Soulful Connection

At the end of each chapter, we offer practical exercises designed to enliven and enrich your marriage. We recommend that Personal Practice exercises be done alone and Soulful Connection exercises be engaged in as a couple. You will find practices for understanding your personality style, managing anger and other emotions, seeing issues from different perspectives, and cultivating compassion and forgiveness for yourself and each other. These are designed to help you reflect on past and present experiences, improve communication, and enhance intimacy. Be sure to set aside time for in-house dates to complete these Soulful Connection activities.

As individuals and as a couple, we have explored the world's religions and many cultural beliefs and practices. We provide a sampling of spiritual practices from various faith traditions. Not everything we offer will be right for you. Allow this diverse presentation to help you clarify your own spiritual belief system. We encourage you to discuss your own religious or spiritual beliefs with your partner. Be willing to make shifts in your consciousness as you learn and grow.

If your marriage is foundering or you have not established a high level of trust, we recommend that you do some of the challenging or confrontational exercises with a professional counselor, coach, or spiritual director.

Some Notes on Style

Since this book is primarily intended for all sincerely committed couples, including same-sex couples and those involved in civil unions, we use the following words interchangeably throughout this book: spouse, partner, mate, dear one, beloved. Also, to avoid gender bias as simply as possible, we alternate between male and female pronouns.

To keep the book accessible to people of all faith traditions, we refer to the Divine as God, Spirit, Universe, Divine, Great Mystery, Creator, or Beloved when referring to the sacred dimension. Please feel free to insert other names for the Sacred if you don't find your chosen name within these pages.

We realize that as coauthors we write very differently and we have decided to let our differences shine through. We outlined each chapter together and worked side by side to write much of the text. However, we also assigned ourselves some separate sections, then edited each other's writing. Both of us made an effort to accommodate the other's writing style. We hope to demonstrate that people who are very different from one another can effectively collaborate to create great books—and wonderful marriages.

Practical Uses for This Book

Feel free to read this book alone or with your mate. Read at your own pace to best grasp and assimilate the material. Writing in a personal or a couple's journal can help you process what you are learning. Jotting down notes, emotional reactions, and breakthroughs may help you gain clarity and develop a sense of excitement about your relationship and your progress. Journaling about the exercises at the end of the chapters may elevate your awareness and clarify your insights. Responses given the first time you try an exercise may be dramatically different from future repeats, after implementing what you have learned. Your journal may be a source of inspiration to continue the process of deepening your love.

Some couples designate a date night to read this book and to do the exercises together. We invite you to frequently engage each other in meaningful and powerful ways, realizing that building your relationship requires rigor and focus, and is not always fun. Ongoing mindfulness, sincerity, and commitment create and sustain your soulful marriage.

You will benefit from reading and working with this book when your relationship is progressing smoothly, as well as when problems arise. You may selectively read topics that speak to you or that are relevant to issues you are facing.

Discussing the chapters and exercises in *Secrets of a Soulful Marriage* with other committed couples in a book club or couples group can deepen everyone's learning. How potentially powerful to join with others as you progress on your journey of living as a soulful couple!

Since growth is usually a gradual process, we suggest that you regularly return to this book to discuss and apply just a few ideas, tools, and practices at a time. If you are working with a counselor, coach, guide, or spiritual director, you may want to let her know about your engagement with *Secrets of a Soulful Marriage*. She can enhance the progress you are making on the path of soulful connection.

The Power of Story

As you pursue your journey to develop a soulful marriage, it is important to remember the beginning, where the relationship started. What is your story? How did you meet? Did your family or friends introduce you? Did you meet online or do you believe your meeting was "arranged" by cosmic forces? Life is so mysterious. What do you each recall about your courtship? Those early experiences of being together provide the foundation of your relationship, and the cornerstones on which you have built your marriage.

Love is often colorful, dramatic, and playful. We have had the pleasure of hearing many thrilling and outrageous stories of how happy couples met. Ours is one such story, which we would like to share to encourage you to recount the magic of your own beginning.

Our Wild Beginning: Jim's Version

In the fall of my senior year of college, my apartment roommate, Alan, asked me to speak on the phone to his sophomore blind date to answer some questions for her about a class that I had previously taken. Although our conversation was fairly brief and ordinary, I had the strange thought that I should be going out with her because I was less than two years older than she was, whereas my roommate was four years older. A week or so later Alan reported briefly meeting her and that she was "nothing special."

The next weekend Alan had his first date with this girl. Neither was enjoying the other, but because the night was young, the girl agreed to come to our apartment to meet my date and me. The two of them intruded on us making out on the couch and we quickly sat up as the door opened. Before Alan had a chance to introduce his date, she brazenly began to critique a collage I had made that was hanging on a wall by the door. Her boldness commanded my attention, as did her liveliness. Alan's date and I began sparking off one another in conversation, while the other two receded into the background. At one point, Alan went into the bedroom to make a phone call and my date went to the bathroom. I then followed the mystery girl into the kitchen after she nervously rose to get a glass of water. Impulsively, I spun her around and kissed her on the lips—a brazen act and something I had never done previously nor repeated. The electricity between us was palpable. The remainder of the evening was a blur to both of us.

You probably realize that Alan's date was Ruth, my bride now of over forty years. Neither of us ever recalled what happened to our dates after my bold *Hello, there!* kiss. I don't even remember taking my date, who was visiting me for the weekend, to the train station. (We had casually dated the previous summer in my hometown.) The only thing I remember was asking Alan if I could ask Ruth out, to which he replied, "You can have her!"

Ruth and I proceeded to have four long, glorious dates that fall of 1967, ranging from dinners to attending football games and a theatrical play, to merely studying together. At one point during our study date in my apartment, the third of the four dates, I took a break to talk with Ruth. As we stood about a foot apart looking into each other's eyes, I was jolted by a sudden, highly mystical experience—I sensed that I was peering into eternity! I had never before (or after) had such an experience. When I called Ruth in mid-December, after this series of dates, she was hopeful that I would ask her out for New Year's Eve. Instead, in the middle of a good conversation, I shocked her and surprised myself by impulsively breaking up with her. Looking back on that instant decision, I am quite sure that I was unconsciously frightened by the prospect of finding my soul mate. Having been rejected a year and a half earlier by a girl whom I had dated for a year and loved, I was not ready for another committed relationship, let alone one of this magnitude.

I did not have any further contact with Ruth until three months later, when I spotted her across a large ballroom floor at a college dance to begin the spring term. Although we were both leery of reconnecting, we conversed and danced together. Two very curious things transpired. First, I called Alan and simply mentioned that Ruth was standing nearby. Alan retorted with conviction, "You're going to marry her," which stunned me, although I dismissed the idea at the time. Second, when I offered to turn the water fountain on for Ruth, she later said that she thought to herself, "If he turns that water off [in midstream], that's it for him!" I kept both the water and our relationship on and we've flowed onward ever since. Despite attending graduate school the next fall about 150 miles away, Ruth and I continued seeing one another every few weekends. We were delighted to be married less than two years later at a large and festive wedding.

Our Wild Beginning: Ruth's Version

After a very frustrating freshman year at Penn State, I was telling a cousin at a summer family event that I was feeling very lonely and disconnected. She suggested I call her fiancé's best friend, Alan, who was studying for his doctorate in psychology at Penn State. I thought, "What? I am just going to be a sophomore. How can I call a doctoral student?" I simply replied, "Thank you" and took the piece of paper with his name and number.

When I returned for the fall term, I tucked the piece of paper away, too nervous to make the call. Finally, in November, I got up enough courage to call. I met Alan for a movie. Alan had no emotional reaction to the fabulous movie *Cool Hand Luke*—and we had no chemistry. Since the night was young, I decided to go to his apartment to meet his roommate and his roommate's date.

As we entered the apartment, the roommate and a girl were kissing on the couch. She sat up quickly, but he lay there beaming at me. My heart flipped and I thought, "He is so cute!" As the night went on, Jim and I were enthralled with each other. We talked, laughed, and flirted. I connected with him more deeply than with anyone I had ever met. The roommate and the other girl simply disappeared!

Jim and I were alone in the living room. I got nervous, so I went into the kitchen for water. Jim followed me, twirled me around, and planted a big kiss on my lips. Although I responded, we were both startled.

To this day, we do not know where the other two people went or how I got back to my dorm. Jim and I shared four engaging dates until winter break. The night before we left for the holidays, Jim called. I thought he would ask me out for New Year's Eve. Instead, he said, "We shouldn't see each other anymore. We are just too different; I just don't think it will work out." I was devastated. I got very sick, missing most of the winter term.

When I returned for spring term, I attended a campus dance. There, across a noisy, crowded room, was Jim Sharon, strolling toward me. Hesitantly, I went into the hall to talk with him. We decided to try it again and happily dated all spring. After Jim graduated, we deepened a long-distance relationship for two years and fell in love. We claimed we had the best relationship in the world. We touched each other on every level and were convinced that being together forever was a gift that would never wear out.

After Jim's American University master's degree in psychology and my Penn State degree in elementary education, we began a new chapter. Reciting our vows under the *chuppah* (the Jewish wedding canopy) and joining as a sacred couple on June 7, 1970, we celebrated in the presence of family, friends, and God. Coincidentally (as if an endorsement or a wink from the Divine), the rabbi who officiated at our wedding was the son of the rabbi who had married Jim's parents twenty-eight years earlier in another state.

Soulful Connection: What Is Your Story?

Take a few moments to retell your story afresh to each other. Share how you each remember the details, sentiments, feelings, and thoughts of your meeting.

Every so often, recount your meeting, dating, deciding to marry, and special events in your relationship. How you tell the story can reveal so much about each of you and who you are as a couple. You can record this meeting story in writing or on video for later generations to enjoy.

Are You Ready to Begin?

Ready to go exploring? We are your trustworthy, capable guides on this expedition into the depths and heights of love and healthy relationship.

You may be traveling this path on your own. Perhaps your spouse is content maintaining your relationship status quo, rather than seeking to grow. Your efforts at new behaviors and commitments can still contribute to the transformation of your relationship. For those who are single and seeking a soulful relationship, this book will help you prepare for your future partner.

For those who are couples embarking on this journey together, consider these questions: Are you willing to share your new insights with your partner along the way so she understands the changes you're making? Will you travel this path as partners, engaged in the process together, step by step? Find what works best for you and your mate. Be aware of your choices and make them as consciously as you can.

> One of the most calming and powerful actions you can do to intervene in a stormy world is to stand up and show your soul ... To display the lantern of soul in shadowy times like these is to be fierce and to show mercy toward others; both are acts of immense bravery and greatest necessity.
>
> —Clarissa Pinkola Estes,
> *You Were Made for This*

Our intention is to share what we have learned without trying to impose our philosophical or spiritual beliefs. Our current belief is that the eternal soul enters into the body and establishes an identity and personality, animates this earthly life, learns lessons, then moves on to other realms or dimensions. Please take what nourishes you, what makes sense for you, and leave the rest. This book is like a banquet table—just take what you can digest. Come back another time. Enjoy the feast and the company!

This is our time in history to reveal our collective secrets, to uncover wisdom as we evolve past our personal story into the collective story. Are you ready to let the lantern of your soul shine to guide the way for your own adventure, for those in your circle of influence, and for future generations? This can be your enduring legacy!

We wish you a glorious journey as you develop skills and attitudes to unfold your potential and to live as a happy person, in partnership with your spouse. As the two of you evolve, you are likely to create powerful and beautiful synergy as a soulful couple.

Getting Personal

Taking on Your Inner Work

Until you make the unconscious conscious, it will direct your life and you will call it fate.

—Carl Jung, *Memories, Dreams, Reflections*

As the saying goes, "A chain is as strong as its weakest link." This is an apt metaphor for marriages. You are able to flourish when both of you participate in creating and sustaining your sacred relationship. Equally important—perhaps even fundamental—is for each of you to focus on your own personal development. When you have a greater sense of who you are, you have a greater ability to give love and receive love.

Are you willing to really face yourself? Will you work to further develop yourself, enabling you to contribute more to your partnership? Are you ready to get down and dirty so you can grow as a person?

In this chapter, you will learn that one of the secrets of a soulful marriage is to recognize how your personal history has shaped you. You each come to the relationship with your bags packed full of your past. We provide you with techniques and perspectives you need to examine what is in your individual bags. You will learn how your past affects your individual life today as well as your partnership now and in the future. As you

1

understand your past, you can be proactive in creating the present and the future you desire. We guide you and your partner to support each other through this work of sorting out past influences, which will ultimately benefit your union.

Self-Esteem: A Building Block for You and Your Relationship

How you act as a romantic partner is strongly affected by your perception of your worth or value as a person. Your self-assessment, which makes up your self-esteem, is based on a combination of attitudes, beliefs, and emotions about your inner and physical nature. A solid sense of yourself is very closely related to self-acceptance and self-love, both of which are keys to sincerely loving others.

When your self-esteem is strong, you are more likely to perceive, and feel worthy of, the good in your life, including receiving the love of another person. You set goals for yourself because you have confidence in your ability to achieve them and you love freely, knowing that you have something valuable to offer another person.

When your self-esteem is low, when you are not able to accept who you are, you are more likely to reject much that is good in your life, including the benefits of a loving relationship, because you do not feel worthy. You may not set personal goals because you lack the confidence to attain them and you may not believe that the love you have to offer has value.

The development of your self-esteem begins very early in life and any challenges to self-esteem can have lasting effects well into adulthood. To poignantly illustrate how your self-esteem can get eroded, imagine that you are born holding a paper sign that reads, I am lovable and capable. Then, starting as a young child, each time you hear a negative remark or judgment about yourself, a piece of your sign gets ripped away.

Consider this example:

Excited to be starting first grade, Jeremy boards the school bus. An older boy sitting near the back spots him and blurts out, "Hey, little shrimp, where did ya get that nerdy haircut?" Rip! During the school day, Jeremy's teacher calls his name, but he does not hear her. In a harsh tone, the teacher reprimands the boy, "Don't you daydream in my class. You need to pay attention here!" Rip! When Jeremy returns home on that rainy afternoon, his mother, already in a bad mood from a trying day, greets him with, "How dare you track mud on the floor and throw your wet jacket on the chair? You are so inconsiderate!" Rip! Young Jeremy had begun the day cheerfully, but by late afternoon, he feels deflated.

How often have you felt diminished by being labeled as lazy, selfish, rude, or stupid? How often have you been rebuked in a hurtful manner? The cumulative effect of various and repeated harsh criticisms or judgments exacts a toll on your self-image. It takes intentional effort to restore your sense of self-worth and to repair your shattered sign.

Shift in Consciousness

Conventional Model: Your Achievements Matter

Your worth as a person depends on your character and achievements, which generally fall short of external standards, such as those of your parents or teachers. Remember how often your wrong answers in school were accentuated by red X's on your papers?

Soulful Model: You Matter

You are intrinsically worthy. Transformation involves shifting models from needing to be perfect and complete to accepting your imperfections and trusting the mystery of life that is continually unfolding. Nobody consistently gets everything right and nobody is perfectly packaged. And what is the standard for perfection—a highly subjective term often determined by someone else's standards—anyway?

The soulful model of self-image recasts our concerns about flaws, as illustrated in a well-known story told here from a Jewish Hasidic perspective, but which is also attributed to Indian, Chinese, and other traditions.

The Cracked Pot: A Story for Anyone Who's Not Quite Perfect

Moshe the water carrier lives in a shtetl. He carries two clay pots on a yoke over his shoulder, and makes many trips a day back and forth from the stream to houses in his neighborhood.

One pot has a small crack, so it leaks slowly. As he walks, water leaks out of the cracked pot. Instead of two full pots, the last delivery gets one and a half pots of water from the stream.

For a full two years this goes on daily, with the water bearer delivering only one and a half pots full of water to the woman at the end of the road.

The perfect pot was proud of its accomplishments, perfect for its mission in life. But the poor cracked pot was ashamed of its own imperfection, and miserable that it was able to accomplish only half of what it had been made to do.

After two years of what it perceived to be a bitter failure, it spoke to the water bearer one day by the stream: "I am ashamed of myself, and I want to apologize to you."

"Why?" asked the water bearer. "What are you ashamed of?"

"I have been able, for these past two years, to deliver only half of my load because this crack in my side causes water to leak out all the way back to your neighbor's house. Because of my flaws, you have to do all this work, and you don't get full value from your efforts," the pot lamented.

The water bearer felt sorry for the old cracked pot, and in his compassion Moshe said, "As we return to the neighbor's house, I want you to notice the beautiful flowers along the path."

Indeed, as they went up the hill, the old cracked pot took notice of the sun warming the beautiful wildflowers on the side of the path, and this cheered it some.

But at the end of the trail, it still felt bad because it had leaked out half its load, and so again it apologized to the bearer for its failure.

Moshe said to the pot, "Did you notice that there were flowers only on your side of the path, but not on the other pot's side? "That's because I have always known about your flaw, and I took advantage of it. I planted flower seeds on your side of the path, and every day while we walk back from the stream, you've watered them.

"For two years I have been able to pick these beautiful flowers to decorate my neighbor's table. If you were not just the way you are, she would not have this beauty to grace her house."

We each have our own unique flaws. We are all "cracked pots" (or crackpots). Our imperfections make our lives together revealing and rewarding. However, even if you generally accept your imperfections, you are likely to feel vulnerable or sensitive about certain aspects of yourself. Some of these vulnerabilities are near the surface and easy to identify. Others may be so deeply internalized that you don't even realize they are there—yet they still underlie your actions and reactions.

It is important to understand your sensitive areas of concern because, even unnoticed, they can lower your self-esteem. Once you have named these vulnerable spots, you are better able to assess their validity and either accept them as part of who you are or set a goal to change them. See the exercises at the end of the chapter to help you begin this process of identifying aspects of yourself you are not happy with.

Self-Inquiry: Taking an Inventory of Yourself

You may be aware of significant changes in the cultural mind-set over recent decades about accepting responsibility for your emotions. Are you coming to realize that expecting your spouse to make you happy leads to resentment and unhappiness? Although your partner may influence your happiness, you are responsible for activating attitudes and behaviors that promote your own feeling of happiness. Self-worth, self-esteem, and loving your life are by-products of your diligence and persistence in removing blocks to your fulfillment. Ultimately, true happiness is an attained state of being that transcends pleasant experiences or transient moods.

Shift in Consciousness

Conventional Model: You Depend on Your Partner

My partner is responsible for making me happy. It is okay for me to blame, shame, judge, and punish my partner for not making me happy.

Soulful Model: You Empower Your Own Happiness

I am responsible for my own happiness. My partner is my well-wisher, assisting me in fulfilling my needs, understanding my feelings, and supporting me in being all that I can be.

Check in with yourself right now. Where you are on the following continuum?

X——————————————————————— X

I have no awareness of   I am freeing myself and

having a personal story.   rewriting my story.

With gentleness and compassion, take time regularly to get to know your-self more fully. Learn to discern your authentic self from the story of who you are, which may have been given to you as a child, by others. A useful starting point is to take inventory of your basic beliefs, values, desires, and goals by reflecting on the following questions:

- Who am I?

- Why am I here?

- What is (are) my primary life purpose(s)?

Contemplating your responses to these vital questions is an ongoing, pow-erful way to develop clarity, life direction, and soulful depth. Take your time with them; you may want to approach these questions during several contemplation sessions. Let your responses be free-flowing to loosen up your thoughts and emotions. Try to work past the usual answers, open-ing up creative streams of new ideas. Pay attention to the sensations or feelings in or around your heart and gut as you respond. Record your responses in a journal and reread them at a later date to add more ideas and uncover deeper layers of awareness.

Follow the basic questions with these inquiries to deepen your inner knowing:

- What are my core values?

- How can I better manage my time, energy, and money?

- What are my big dreams or what are my bucket-list priorities
  (what I want to be sure that I accomplish during my lifetime)?

See page 13 for a similar exercise to do with your partner.

Inner Work for the Soulful Marriage: Chris and Sylvia

Chris: My inner work is simply the conscious journey of awakening toward the "Grand Awakening." I chose to partner with Sylvia, who is also seeking to spiritually awaken. En route to our Grand Awakening, many stepping-stones have appeared. Truth has been revealing itself on more profound levels over the thirty-six years of our marriage.

Throughout our journey, we periodically ask ourselves, "Are we still destined to travel together?" After all, we grow at different paces. Priorities change and life's challenges bend and shape us day in and day out. I know that to continue being with Sylvia *and* have ongoing awakenings, I must explore my inner depths. The risk of migrating from soul mates to cell-mates becomes a possibility.

Our soulful union as a couple is amazing. If one stumbles, the other supports. When one experiences great joy, the other celebrates the wonder.

Sylvia: Transcendence is the touchstone for our staying connected. We cannot be today what we were a year ago. Being in a relationship, life continuously calls us to grow and change, to share our values and mutually evolve. For my own spiritual development, I embrace transparency, coherence, and wholeness. Life with my partner beckons me to be passionate and full of joy. Wherever attention goes is where the heart is. Ultimately, love transforms us. Chris and I are here to share in love, to be love, and, in that, we are one.

Growth Can Be Chaotic

Deep inner work tends to be challenging and rigorous. Realize that personal growth often occurs slowly and is not linear. It can feel chaotic when you are in the thick of it. As you have experienced many times during your life, you encounter setbacks or reversals along the way.

Personal growth can be sparked by an event or a series of events that may be extremely painful, such as the loss of a loved one, either by relocation, relationship breakup, or death; a near-death experience or a life-threatening illness; the loss of a career, financial distress, or the loss of your home; admission of your own or your partner's addiction or infidelity.

The push for personal development may also result from happy occasions, like a marriage, a move, a promotion, a new business, the birth of a baby, adopting or raising a child or children, a new opportunity, a successful venture, an inheritance, or winnings.

Although chaos may feel overwhelming, it can sometimes prompt positive growth. As an example, Marsha and Sandy, who were high school sweethearts, parted ways, married others, and had not had contact for many years. Both being widowed, they connected again through family ties, and have now been married for more than twelve years.

When you encounter intense or rapid change, you may feel anxious, confused, disoriented, depressed, or in pain. If this is your experience, fasten your seat belt for a potentially bumpy ride across unfamiliar terrain. Several examples of what you or your partner might experience during major periods of growth, especially growth prompted by rapid change, are:

Physical:

- Changing appetite and sleeping patterns

- Feeling disoriented, spacy, or perhaps even dizzy

- Needing to be alone, away from crowds, electronics, intense lighting

Emotional:

- Feeling deeply sad or melancholy for no apparent reason

- Craving solitude, despite previously being more sociable; feeling lonely or lost in a crowd

- Losing passion for life; previously enjoyable activities or relationships may no longer interest you

Mental:

- Focusing internally; more self-talk as new realizations or insights emerge

- Witnessing a dramatic increase in intuitive abilities

- Comprehending information more rapidly and/or at a deeper level

Spiritual:

- Yearning for clarity about the meaning of life and about your purpose on earth

- Sensing a deep longing to be in spiritual company, read, pray, meditate

- Noticing more coincidences or synchronous events that may startle or amaze you

Do any of these responses sound familiar? Everyone experiences transformation differently. Avoid judging yourself or your partner. Have compassion for what you and your beloved are enduring. As the saying goes, "This too shall pass."

Stay Tuned and Stay in Tune

Often in life one door (or opportunity) closes and another door (or opportunity) opens. Trusting your resourcefulness and remaining optimistic are helpful attitudes for navigating through personal growth. Embracing periods of descent and ascent, the dark and the light, are essential for becoming whole. Growing into the fullness of who you are is an ongoing process, a lifelong journey.

Understand that the journey involves gradually uncovering your best qualities, rather than a total personality makeover. Amid the growing pains, stretch your comfort zone—get braver, clearer, more empowered and impassioned. Are you willing to become strong enough to avoid resistance to growing?

Here is some simple stress management imagery that may prove useful to you as you grow stronger:

Imagine your body as a paper cup filled with water, representing the life force. When your cup is full, you are filled with life energy. Your insecurities and external stressors act like pins, poking holes in the cup. As water drains out of the cup, you might feel depleted, helpless, and powerless. However, you have the power to seal the holes in the leaky cup and to prevent further pinholes from occurring by strengthening the walls of your cup. As you grow more resilient, your sealed vessel is able to hold more life energy, making you more present, more available, more masterful, and better able to love and be loved.

When you and your partner each take responsibility to seal the leaks in your personal vessel, your relationship has a greater chance of flourishing. When you feel you have some control over the stressors sapping your energy, your mind is likely to become quieter, your body may feel more relaxed, and your disposition seems calmer. As these favorable effects occur, you can often gain a better sense of what really matters to you. With this clearer perspective, you are better able to articulate your feelings to your partner and better able to listen as he shares his intentions and goals.

Inevitably, you and your partner experience personal growth at different paces and rhythms. One of you might have a slow, steady rhythm. Perhaps the other will experience a large growth spurt and then withdraw for a while to process the experience. Remaining in communication is essential. Learn how to articulate what is going on and what you need from your partner. For example, "I just feel so grouchy lately, as you've noticed. I don't know what is going on. I simply need to rest and be quiet for a while. I will talk to you after my nap, okay?" Beware of assuming, defending, blaming, and disconnecting.

Taking responsibility for your own feelings and needs gives you more power and choices in your life. You may feel wonderful when you are in the midst of a growth surge; you may also feel vulnerable or exposed. Allow yourself a period of adjustment to your new ways of thinking, feeling, and behaving. Some people report these kinds of thoughts or feelings:

- "What is going on with me?"
- "I don't know which way to turn anymore."
- "I feel as if I'm in free fall."
- "All the rules have changed; I don't know how to act."
- "What could possibly happen next?"
- "Am I going nuts?"

One positive approach to personal development is to welcome these experiences as learning opportunities, viewing them as aha moments and flashes of new awareness. Keep your perspective and sense of humor as much as you can.

Ask your partner for support. As you proceed in your journey of uncovering and discovering what makes you tick, you become more of who you are. Many names have been used to refer to this unfolding and evolution of your essence: self-realization, enlightenment, awakening your soul, and emanating your Truth, Godliness, Sacred Goddess, Higher Self, Christ-consciousness, or Buddha nature.

Are you sufficiently motivated to forge ahead? Gain inspiration from the instructive story of R. U. Darby, which Napoleon Hill relates in his classic book, *Think and Grow Rich*.

Three Feet from Gold

Darby's uncle had gold fever, so he staked his claim and started digging. After much hard work, the uncle found a vein of ore, which he covered up, then came home to raise funds needed to buy machinery for unearthing the ore. Upon collecting the money, Darby and his uncle excitedly returned to the site, fully expecting to soon strike it rich.

As the two men resumed digging, more ore initially surfaced. However, despite their persistent digging, the gold supply suddenly ceased. Deeply frustrated and disappointed, they abandoned their efforts and sold their machinery to a junk man for a pittance.

The astute junk man hired a mining engineer, who checked the mine and calculated that a vein of gold lay just three feet below where Darby and his uncle had stopped digging. The junk man proceeded to earn millions from that mine.

The story also had a happy ending for Darby. Determined to learn his lesson from quitting early, he persevered to such an extent as an insurance salesman that he became more successful than he would have been with the gold sales.

During turbulent times, remember that you, like Darby, may be just three feet from gold—or you may ultimately discover a more fulfilling path.

Here's a top-secret tip. The purest gold that you can mine can be found less than three inches inside your skin—your own heart! You need not be a miner or an Olympian to go for the gold.

Hopefully, you now have an expanded perspective of the double-edged-sword nature of growth work. While the process may be tedious, painful, and challenging, your persistence pays dividends—a great investment in your future as an individual and as part of a soulful couple. You have the potential to thrive. As you do, you exert a positive influence on your spouse and your partnership.

This chapter has offered you the opportunity to become more aware of factors or events that have shaped your personality. You have also explored the nature of the growth process and the challenges associated with personal development. In the next chapter, you practice methods for releasing negative behavior patterns that have not served you or your spouse. Share the secret that you can create a richer, more enlivening relationship by transforming your attitudes and skills.

TAKING ACTION

Personal Practice: Rewriting Disturbing Messages

As an adult you still carry the rips and tears of your childhood, and they still hurt. The emotional weight of these negative influences may be lowering your self-esteem.

In your journal, list some particularly painful or upsetting messages from your parents, teachers, peers, and others that you have internalized and considered as true. For example, your aunt would regularly bump into you and call you clumsy. For years, you thought that you indeed were clumsy or a klutz. Perhaps you have come to realize that you are actually graceful and balanced. She was the one who had trouble with spatial relations!

Complete these sentences with several of your strong childhood memories or impressions:

- I was told I was ...

- I believed I was ...

- I now regard myself as ...

How much does each of these messages still affect you? What do you tell yourself that further undermines your self-esteem? For each of the items that you list, counter your hurt with a few statements that dispute the validity of any negative messages that you received. For example:

"I was told I had no athletic ability, but I run five miles a day, five days a week. I'd certainly consider that an athletic achievement."

"I was told that I would never amount to anything, but two generations of kids have graduated from my classroom. I have many boxes

of letters from former students thanking me for being such a positive influence in their lives."

Whether or not you've ever articulated these negative messages in your
relationship, your partner may intentionally or unintentionally exploit these
vulnerabilities. What are some ways in which your partner reinforces what
you were told as a child? What specifically does your mate say or do that
reactivates your hurt?

You may want to share your experience of this exercise with your partner. Explain to your mate that her being aware of and sensitive to these
vulnerabilities will help you in your work to overcome their lasting hurt and
help you heal the old wounds. You can choose to limit how upset you become and you can decide to respond in an effective manner. Healthy ways
to respond and communicate are described in chapter 3. Sometimes, you
can surprise your partner by thanking him for giving you the opportunity to
reduce your reactivity. The overall goal is to respond with awareness rather
than reacting defensively.

Soulful Connection: Key Questions with Your Partner

Arrange a time to walk or sit while you discuss the three questions below.
Take a few deep breaths, clear away distractions, attune to each other with
eye contact, hand-holding, or other physical touch.

Focus on your relationship needs, desires, and areas of improvement.
Take turns asking and answering the following questions, one question at
a time:

- How can I help you to know yourself better?
- How can I be more genuine with you?
- How can I more graciously receive from you *and* in what ways can
  I give more of myself?

Be patient with yourself in responding to your partner. Take time and space
to practice introspection, to assimilate feedback from your partner, and to
be conscious of qualities you want to emanate. Make up your own questions. Conversations grounded in truth deepen or expand the trust and intimacy between you. Jot down notes to help you remember any plans or
agreements that may emerge from your conversation.

Soulful Connection: Supporting Each Other's Well-Being

Meet with your beloved in a quiet place where you can both concentrate undisturbed for thirty to forty-five minutes. Read through the list on page 8 together. Notice which items may describe you at this time.

Discuss how you can support each other physically, emotionally, mentally, and spiritually. Make a plan to meet again in a week or two to evaluate your supportive efforts and acceptance of the support, and to determine what else you may need.

Breaking Loose

Replacing Unwanted Habits with Positive Patterns

Re-examine all you have been told ... Dismiss what insults your soul.
—Walt Whitman, *Leaves of Grass*

A friend once said, "An arrow can only be shot by pulling it backward. So when life is dragging you back with difficulties, it means that it's going to launch you into something great. Just focus and keep aiming."

Sometimes the work of improving your relationship with your loved one, of elevating your partnership to a soulful union, can feel as if you are being pulled backward. And, in a sense, you are. As we learned in the last chapter, part of strengthening your relationship is identifying who you truly are as an individual, and that involves examining your past to determine what experiences made lasting imprints on your attitudes and behaviors. You want to nurture the effects of your positive influences, of course, but you also want to rid your life of the negative patterns that can sabotage your personal growth as an individual and a soulful partner.

In this chapter, we will show you secrets to help you break free from habits that are keeping you from bringing your authentic self into your relationship and into your life.

Becoming Aware of Your Patterns

We all bring preestablished behavior patterns, both positive and negative, into our relationships. Some of these habits or responses were programmed by human evolution, some were formed when we were young through influence and experience, and some are mirrored responses from people around us. Many times we are completely oblivious to them until someone points them out or something affects us that cannot be ignored.

Some of our behavior patterns are shaped by our experiences with others and how they reacted to us. For example, as a child you were highly influenced by authority figures, such as parents, teachers, coaches, and clergy. The amount of encouragement and support you received from others influenced your ability to think for yourself and trust your instincts and feelings. If you were frequently criticized and shamed, you most likely erected some tough walls to help you cope. If this sounds like you, you probably use the same rigid forms of self-protection in your adult life today. This might translate into an overall lack of trust of others or an inability to trust your own emotions.

Other common models of behavior are more primitive, programmed into the area of the brain from which spring our emotions, behavior, and long-term memory, and are intended to keep us safe. Our fight-flight-freeze reactions are adaptive patterns that most people—and animals, too—have in response to life challenges. When faced with danger, stressors, conflicts, or trauma, we tend to react with aggression, avoidance, or immobilizing fear—like a deer in the headlights. Recent research conducted by Dr. Shelley Taylor and her team at the University of California at Los Angeles identified another common trend with primitive roots, mainly demonstrated by women, known as "tend and befriend." During times of stress, women typically react by protecting their young (tending) and seeking out a social group for mutual defense and support (befriending).[1]

Whichever survival mechanism you typically react with, you also unconsciously model behavior patterns of your parents and close relatives. You may be surprised at how much you act, sound, and gesture like your relatives. For example, a client recently mentioned that he was dismayed to realize that he had adopted his father's brand of cynicism and poor hygiene habits. As these patterns slowly become ingrained in your brain, you may be unaware of their effect on your current relationship.

Take a moment to listen to what you are yakking about in your head, that inner conversation often referred to as self-talk. Do you hear new, original thoughts or can you picture the same words being said by someone else in your life? Do you hear the oh-so-familiar tape loops continuously going around in your head?

Now think back on some of your current and past conversations with your partner. Do you sound like a broken record sometimes? How frustrating to be caught in the web of same old, same old within yourself and with your partner. Repetitive patterns can lead to dullness and fatigue. You become resigned to an unsatisfying way of communicating, which can result in depression. You may settle into a trancelike state and be barely present to enjoy your partner, your work, or your life in general.

You can choose to awaken from the trance, embrace the present moment, and restore vitality and positive possibilities to all aspects of your life, including your relationship. Becoming aware of your negative patterns of reactions is the first step in letting them go. As you develop healthier, more intentional emotional responses, you are likely to feel happier and to bring that positive energy into your marriage.

Blind spots or lack of awareness are part of the human condition, so it may be useful to encourage your partner to help you identify your negative patterns, and to encourage him to identify his. Be kind when you let your partner know you may have found one of his blind spots, and be receptive when your partner points out yours. Learn to recognize the verbal and nonverbal feedback that your mate gives you. Realize, however, that your mate is only sharing his perceptions, some of which may be distorted. It is often useful to seek counsel from an objective professional when doing this important work. Conflicts may flare up if you don't handle these kinds of exchanges with care, patience, and compassion.

As you become clear about your individual and shared patterns, you have more power to create the relationship you each truly want. Knowing that both of you are becoming more focused on making favorable changes can lead to a more trusting and soulful connection. Even if only one of you is leading the way in this process, there can be a positive impact on your partnership, establishing a newfound respect and love for each other.

Healing a Difficult Relationship: Kathy

I felt trapped in a negative relationship with my husband, Tom. I continually found fault with him and picked on his inadequacies. I became obsessed with proving that I was better than Tom in so many ways. As my bitterness intensified, I became very ill and sought counseling to help restore my marriage and my health.

While discussing my preoccupation with demeaning Tom, my counselor interrupted my tirade with a simple question: "Is this how you tend to treat others?" I suddenly had a rush of memories of acting stuck up and nasty to several classmates during middle school. Yuk, this pattern of being superior to others has been with me a long time. Now I recognize my choice: shrinking in shame or expanding my perceptions of myself and forgiving my judgmental style. I made a decision to disengage from this unhealthy habit of incessantly finding fault with my husband.

Using imagery, I view my body as a sacred vessel. I clean, clear, and purify my inner sanctuary. I am learning powerful ways of healing the pain that I have carried for over thirty years. As I practice healing methods on my own, I am becoming kinder and more respectful toward my husband. In the process, I feel a new sense of confidence and ease. My emotions are more positive. I feel centered and calm more of the time. My health is better and my marriage is more grounded.

Understanding Codependency and Aiming for Interdependency

Healthy personal development unfolds in four main stages of behavior: dependency, codependency, independence, and interdependency. When you were a baby, you were totally dependent on your caregivers to satisfy your basic needs. As a child, you became more independent, even though you still relied on your parents to meet many of your basic needs. Ideally, as you grew, you gradually separated from your parents to become fully independent. When you enter into a healthy relationship, you become interdependent. This means that you and your partner mutually support and empower each other in achieving your individual and collective goals throughout your daily lives.

Relationships suffer when interdependency is thwarted—when one or both partners revert to a negative kind of codependency. This adult form of codependency is apparent when the thoughts and actions of one person revolve around another person. This kind of codependency often results from lack of a strong sense of personal identity. Simply stated, being codependent, in its adult form, means basing your self-worth on others' perception of you. If you base your self-image on what others think of you, your mantra sounds like this: "How do I have to act to get you to validate, like, and love me?"

Continually vying for control and struggling for decision-making power also characterize codependent relationships. Addiction and abuse amplify these reactive patterns and stunt healthy development. Sometimes addiction occurs for many generations. Adult children of alcoholics often have great difficulty maintaining intimate and stable relationships. Codependent tendencies surface in most families; the choice to become more interdependent is an important key to cultivating a soulful relationship.

To assess your codependency tendencies, take the "What Is Your Codependency Score?" survey at the end of this chapter. Without a clear sense of who you are, you may suffer from low self-esteem, a fear of being true to yourself, and minimal confidence in expressing your genuine feelings and needs. This is hardly a solid foundation for a healthy relationship, let alone a soulful one.

Our Greatest Gifts: Amy and Matthew

Two beautiful souls roaming through life, on a mission to love and change the world, we met in an altered state. Living life as party companions and as best friends, we graduated from college, moved to Denver, and married. Everything shifted when we found out that Elijah, our precious gift, had been conceived.

Amy: I quickly stepped up to the challenges of motherhood, fighting through temptations to party for the sake of our unborn son. Matthew quit drinking beer but increased his consumption of hard liquor, drinking secretly. Our marriage became a litany of lies and fights. I would yell, "I wish I'd never married you, an alcoholic!"

Matthew: I knew I was an alcoholic. Infected with the disease through nature and nurture, alcohol had been running through my veins since I was fourteen years old.

Amy: Our life became unmanageable. In the darkness of delusion, we both felt alone and empty.

An angel in a therapist's body stepped into our lives. He brought truth, love, and hope. After a weeklong binge, everyone, including Matthew, agreed that it was time. Matthew entered a thirty-day inpatient rehab program. We grew independently, Matthew through the twelve-step program and Amy with therapy.

Amy and Matthew: As time went by, trust and truth entered our hearts. Growth became an everyday theme. As we began to heal, confidence rose, and love was flowing. Our family found a place to explore our spiritual nature. With the support of years of classes, worship services, and incessant prayers, we began to believe in each other and in a Power greater than ourselves.

Being best friends has ultimately been the greatest gift. We are on a never-ending journey to love and to serve all of life. Admitting when we are wrong and working to resolve problems as they come up, we openly communicate and expand our vision, as individuals, as a couple, as a family! We are love, creativity, flowing, and trusting as One!

Programs, groups, and individual support professionals are readily available, and being humble enough to ask for help is an important step in recovery from codependency, whether substance abuse is implicated or not. Many people are raised to avoid asking for help directly because being vulnerable can be uncomfortable. Instead, you manipulate others by acting childishly helpless or serve as the dominant, do-it-all partner. These covert patterns restrict the ability to maturely love another human being.

As you can tell, we share the good news and the bad news—the expansive and the restrictive. The main message we hope you take away is that you have a choice in the matter. Being aware is your power tool to use!

Shift in Consciousness

Conventional Model: Supporting Codependency

Many of you probably have received some version of these messages: "Think, feel, and act similar to me so that we both can stay safe, comfortable, and connected. If you dare to be different from me, you will jeopardize our relationship and possibly risk losing my love."

Soulful Model: Cultivating Interdependency

Have you been fortunate to receive messages like these? "I encourage you to discover your uniqueness and to express your authentic self in our relationship and in the world. I accept our differences and trust that we can constructively resolve conflicts that arise. We give strength and well-being to each other through our love and respect."

Shifting from old, programmed behaviors to new, more conscious responses gives you skills in relating well with your partner. You become aware that you are not stuck in an unfulfilling pattern, but instead have the power to change and evolve.

Friend or Foe?

For better or for worse, you bring your entire self into your marriage: your history, character, beliefs, personality, habits, family, and more. You have been shaped by family perceptions and models, as well as by the down-loaded messages from your environment. The culture and the times in which you live color your identity and your relationship.

When you are rested and feeling confident, you are likely to be more open-minded and your partner is much more likely to appear as your friend than when you are stressed, depleted, cranky, and defensive. When you are under pressure, your precious friend may look like your foe. And if you feel that your mate is opposing you, you are likely to defend, strategize, manipulate, or attack—and to suffer the consequences.

Think about it: When your partner makes requests for you to change patterns of negative behavior, do you typically dig in your heels and defend yourself, or are you willing to listen to and consider the request? If it is presented and received with the right intention, your partner's request becomes an opportunity for personal growth. Perhaps he sees something in you that you do not perceive. Allow him to support you as you evolve.

What if you indeed interpreted your partner's request to change as a gift coming from your lover, a person who wants you to thrive together? Here is an illustrative scenario. As a corporate executive, mother of three, and active volunteer, Heather is constantly on the go and accepting virtually every request made of her. Heather initially reacted defensively when her husband, Jason, pointed out that her nonstop activity and difficulty saying no were overstressing her, affecting her health, and limiting quality time with him and the family. She claimed that she is a very caring, dedicated, and competent person who honors her responsibilities. But following a discussion with Jason, when she had time to reflect, Heather came to realize that she could be more efficient and effective in every phase of her life by taking periodic breaks each day, by scheduling some personal time, by relaxing with the family on weekends, and by turning down some project and volunteer requests. Within two weeks of implementing these changes, Heather felt her energy replenished and was delighted to observe that she had not compromised her diligence in any area of her life.

> We are here to awaken from the illusion of our separateness.
>
> —Thich Nhat Hanh,
> *Going Home: Jesus and Buddha as Brothers*

Accepting your mate's prompt to consider reevaluating an aspect of your life could initiate a powerful, yet gradual process, so stay patient and committed. Be brave enough, even in the face of fear of the unknown, to enter the unfamiliar territory of humility, vulnerability, and intimacy. Discern what is helpful for implementing change and what keeps you stuck or holds you hostage. A caring and supportive home environment—one that is open, honest, and proactive—nurtures both of you.

Navigating Differences: Carl and Donna

We are not the first couple in a long-term interracial relationship to have noticed that the difference in our personalities plays a greater role than race. The biggest divide between us is extroversion and introversion. As a typical introvert, Carl has much more need for quiet time than I do.

I, on the other hand, get satisfaction from interacting with people and learning in social environments. In the early phases of our relationship, I would take Carl's withdrawal personally, believing that he had lost interest, which made me feel angry and hurt. Being an extrovert, I would talk to him about feeling rejected by the distance. Often he would respond by moving toward me with reassurance. Over time I learned that he always came back and the distance was not a threat or punishment.

What has fortified the bond, despite our differences, is a commitment to talk through what each of us is experiencing. We've often used humor as an effective icebreaker to get conversation back on track. We learned to share our inner reactions without making the other person feel wrong. I often know by the look on Carl's face that one more night out at an event is going to compromise our sense of connection. Conversely, he knows that too much control of my freedom pushes me away. Over time, my need for quiet has increased and Carl has become more social. I believe our relationship has provided the safety to be authentic and to experiment with personal development, often inspired by the other.

Shift in Consciousness

Conventional Model: The 50-50 Split

I will do my 50 percent in our marriage if you give your 50 percent.

During counseling sessions with couples, especially in the early stages, at least one person often says something like this: "I'd be willing to do my part if he would do his." Essentially, such a statement represents a cop-out—one partner expects the other to take the lead, responsibility, or initiative for self-improvement and for enhancing the relationship. This stance allows each of them to renounce his or her power and to blame or shame the other.

Soulful Model: Giving 100 Percent

Our relationship clearly works best when each of us accepts full responsibility for our own attitudes, feelings, needs, and behaviors.

Many marital myths have promoted the value of being 50-50 in a relation-ship. Modern wisdom shows a more enlightened way for each partner in the relationship to be 100 percent responsible for how you create and sustain your union.

Are you willing to declare, "I am all-in! I am willing to be accountable for myself," independent of your partner's attitudes and actions? How powerful! When both you and your partner practice self-responsibility, the potential for synergy is strong. In other words, your combined efforts can have a greater positive effect than if just one of you focused on accepting responsibility.

Here are a few easy sentences to incorporate into your conversations with your partner to help you identify and take responsibility for negative emotional flare-ups when you're interacting. More communication tips and skills can be found in chapter 3.

"When you ..., I feel ..."

"When you do ..., I react ... "

"When you treat me ..., I want to ..."

Share with each other how you feel when you communicate this way. Can you clear away the old patterns of communicating, forgive yourself and your partner for negative ways of behaving, and experience each other a bit more authentically? Can you sense your heart softening more and let-ting more love flow between you and all around you?

Forgiving: A Gateway to Self-Expansion and Real Connection

Many people struggle with what forgiveness means as well as how to for-give. A common misconception is that forgiveness includes exonerating unacceptable behavior.

In a nutshell, forgiveness involves a decision of the heart. In choos-ing to forgive, you compassionately release your harsh judgment without having to condone the undesirable or disturbing behavior. You determine that you will stop using your attitudes and judgments to punish the per-son who upset you. Even if you no longer interact with that person, by forgiving you clear away your own stored emotions and resentments so that you can get on with your life.

The word *forgive* is composed of the words *for* and *give*. When you forgive, you effectively create space for compassionate understanding and perhaps also for a new relationship opportunity.

Forgiveness usually entails a gradual—sometimes very slow—process of letting go of anger or rage, resentment, hurt, and disappointment. Forgiving yourself and others can become a healing balm for the heart. As you heal your pain and can truly open your heart, you are likely to discover the expansive quality of forgiveness.

Discussing painful topics with your partner may open the doors to forgiveness—even slightly—but beware of getting caught in the nasty cycle of "I cannot forgive you until you apologize ... I cannot feel close to you until I forgive you ... I cannot forgive you until I feel connected." Or "I would forgive you, but you have built your walls so high that you cannot accept an apology."

These power struggles are ego-based and are fed by fear. They often involve a resistance to breaking loose from old patterns of thinking and responding. In these discussions, if you find you are becoming increasingly upset, make an agreement to take a break. Each of you can take a time-out to breathe, settle down, and get clear on what you are feeling and what you need. Pay attention to the self-talk in your mind, the feelings in your heart, and the tension in your gut. Then resume talking a short time later. Remind your partner that you want to get along and get past this upset as soon as you can. Remember your love. Renew your promises to work things out and to build a strong relationship.

> Compassionate action has to start with ourselves. It is unconditional compassion for ourselves that leads naturally to unconditional compassion for others.
>
> —Pema Chödrön, *The Places That Scare You: A Guide to Fearlessness in Difficult Times*

Oftentimes, you will revisit the same topics of conflict again and again. Cycles or spirals do not mean that you are regressing or are not right for each other. Learn to replenish your forgiveness reservoir, so that you can draw from it when a troubling situation occurs again. Remind yourself, "Oh, yes, I already forgave her for that. I can let it go now." When you are faced with a challenge, strive for resolution by communicating more, accepting each other's differences, and forgiving each other for things you may have done to hurt each other. Take good care of yourself and manage your stress levels so that you are better equipped to resolve issues more quickly and more effectively. Practicing self-love is also essential for filling your forgiveness reservoir and expanding your heart space.

If the conflict or discomfort does not get resolved immediately, be patient and continue the conversation at a prearranged time. Be clear where you are in the process, so that you can resume it again later at the same point. Be sure to speak from *I*, not the accusatory *you*, to pinpoint the source of the conflict; you are expressing your feelings and your needs. Refer to the communication tools in chapter 3 for more guidance.

At the conclusion of these discussions, thank each other for delving into a difficult topic and for being vulnerable and honest. Acknowledge each other verbally and nonverbally. Hugs and smiles work wonders.

Our Secret Is Never Stop Talking: Kronda and Jamie

We knew from the beginning that we wanted our relationship to extend beyond the fanciful dreams of youth. We had both been in long-term relationships before. Two weeks after we began dating, Jamie jokingly asked Kronda to marry her. Ironically, we had our wedding ceremony exactly five years after Jamie's playful proposal. We were young when we met and young when we married. Through those years we struggled to overcome conventional roles—sharing responsibilities, sharing blame for arguments. Our largest argument centered around who did what—whether housework and college homework equaled eight or more hours at the office. Who should do the dishes was our main point of contention.

> Success is not determined by the outcome. The outcome is the result of having already decided that you are successful to begin with.
>
> —T. F. Hodge, *From Within I Rise: Spiritual Triumph over Death and Conscious Encounters with the Divine Presence*

Three years into our relationship, we found ourselves unable to resolve our ongoing bickering without some external intervention. Neither of us sought direct counseling, but at a seminar we were attending someone happened to mention a book that explained differences in partners' love styles or preferences (*Five Love Languages* by Gary Chapman).

After reading Chapman's book, we became more accepting of each other's personalities and interests. Also, we started setting goals together and talking about things like budgets and plans. Kronda brought work complaints home less frequently. We realized that we needed to be our best selves at home; then work and school would take care of themselves. We still struggle, as all human beings do. But we never stop talking.

Deciding: Being Present and Proactive

As you work through this book, you are engaging in the hard task of identifying negative reaction patterns and habits and learning how to break free from them. Now, with new pathways before you, how do you decide which way to go forward? The answer is to decide moment by moment. You do have free will and the ability to take a stand for what you truly want for yourself and in your relationship. As you've learned throughout this chapter, you choose how to think, speak, or act. Healing old hurts and releasing grudges can clear the way toward forming new attitudes and positive behavior patterns. As with awareness and forgiveness, such changes usually occur gradually. However, the more emotionally open you are through healing, and through forgiving, the greater opportunity you have to access new choices.

When facing decisions, it is important to be fully present in the moment. As you do the healing work to become your most authentic self, your mind may be quieter, your body calmer, and your will more disciplined and determined. You may listen a little more deeply. You may tune in to your inner guidance in clearer ways. Some people hear words or sounds, others see images, or feel feelings or body sensations. Sometimes it is instinctual, something you just know. How do you attune to your inner wisdom?

Decisions in each moment come from your inner values and commitments. As a simple, yet strong example, if you are determined to hold your ground no matter what, you relate to your spouse very differently than if you value being genuinely considerate of her viewpoint. What do you stand for?

The word *decide* comes from the root *de-cise*, meaning "to cut away." Learn to cut away what does not work anymore and make room for new ways of being and behaving. Allow your relationship to reflect your conscious intentions and your heart's desire. (See the Soulful Connection exercise "Regarding Our Relationship ..." on page 37.)

It is difficult and frustrating to make decisions to move forward if you are stuck replaying old dramas, rather than truly listening to each other.

> As you dissolve into love, your ego fades. You're not thinking about loving; you're just love, radiating like the sun.
>
> —Ram Dass, *Be Love Now: The Path of the Heart*

During one of these episodes, you could just decide to do something else. That is what Jim did. "I still recall a brief period fourteen years into our marriage when Ruth and I were engaging in daily trivial fights. One night, during one of those silly arguments, I went to the bathroom. While I was out of the room, I clearly realized that I wanted to effectively interrupt our verbal sparring. When I returned to the bedroom, I spontaneously and gently asked, 'May I give you a foot massage?' Surprised by my disarming offer, Ruth's jaw dropped and she softly replied, 'Okay.' My simple gesture totally disrupted our cycle of arguing. We restored clear communication and resumed enjoying one another."

Isn't it wonderful to know that you have free will and you can choose ways to effect the changes you want? When you know clearly what you stand for, you can make everyday and long-term decisions and take the appropriate actions. When you break free from habitual ways of thinking, speaking, and acting, you reclaim the power of your choices. How freeing it is to be aware of your behavior, to forgive your and others' unhealthy reactions, and to make decisions based on what best serves you and your partner.

Safety versus Growth, Fear versus Love

Take into consideration the need for safety—old habits and familiar behaviors—and the need for growth—fresh responses and authentic action—on a continuum like this:

Safety ——————————————————**Growth**

When these driving forces pull against each other inside you and in your relationship, you experience a conflict of needs. Sometimes it is difficult to decide how to be or what to do because of this dynamic. "Should I pick the safe choice—my usual pattern of behavior—to avoid pain, remain captive to my fears, and maybe regret this path? Or should I take risks by exploring the unfamiliar, open up, go for pleasure, and expand in love?" Hard choices. What if you could bend the above line around to make a circle and realize that at times you are prone to want more safety (roots) and at times you strive to grow and expand (wings). You need the balance of roots and wings to be a highly effective person and to be a partner in a soulful relationship. Learning to listen to your wise inner guide can help you discern the right course. Ask and be attentive.

Safety and growth needs can also be thought of in terms of the driving forces of fear and love. In the book *In His Own Write*, John Lennon said,

> There are two basic motivating forces: fear and love. When we are afraid, we pull back from life. When we are in love, we open to all that life has to offer with passion, excitement, and acceptance. We need to love ourselves first, in all our glory and our imperfections. If we cannot love ourselves, we cannot fully open to our ability to love others, or our potential to create. Evolution and all hopes for a better world rest on the fearlessness and openhearted vision of people who embrace life.[2]

Do you realize that fear often masks what matters most? Learn to convert your fears into loving thoughts, words, and actions. Practice shifting from a trait in the fear column to one attributed to love and watch the miracles unfold.

FEAR	LOVE
control	allow
constrict	open
tighten	relax
worry	trust
separate	unify

As you build the willpower to shift your choices in any moment from fear reactions to love responses, your words and actions reflect your love.

Act: Solve the Problem and Build the Relationship

You can break loose from old patterns and build new pathways in the brain for your evolving self-image and for what is possible as a couple. Inevitably, however, you run into obstacles—these too can be overcome. Keep picturing how you want to be, act, and respond. Run the projector of your mind with the movie in which you envision yourself as the star. The more you visualize what you want, the more the pathway clears before you. Choosing sacred, soulful connection brings about very different actions than trying to protect and defend your ego's rigid position and beliefs. Do you choose fear or love? How about being safe *and* growing?

As you face a conflict with your partner, do your best to clarify the problem and your opposing positions on the issue before trying to resolve it. Very often couples fight about something and realize they actually agree but have not been listening to each other. Find the common ground, such as "We both agree that ... and we are having trouble reconciling our differences about ..."

For example, a couple recently sought coaching for help with their reactive hot buttons with each other. They uncovered the pattern of their fighting and then came up with this solution that reunited them. The woman committed to planning ahead with her husband about what they were wearing to outings, rather than trying to control her husband's choice of clothing through insults and withdrawing from him on their date because he wore the wrong shoes. The man declared he would not dump a pile of his grievances on his wife, which hurt her greatly, but instead would communicate his needs as small conflicts arose. He agreed to use a kind voice, eye contact, and hand-holding as he spoke. They are practicing these new action steps to build the kind of relationship they truly desire.

Think of a current situation in which you are uncertain about what to do. Ask your spouse to be your witness to help you discern your truth. Set a time and place to have this dialogue. Get comfortable. Your partner asks you these questions, then just listens to your answers.

- What situation is weighing on you now?

- What decision are you trying to make?

- Tell me your thoughts and feelings.

- What do you plan to do?

- How can I support you?

How do you feel sharing this way with your partner? Thank her for being present to help you sort out which actions to take. Being a mirror or sounding board is a gift.

Experience the power to interrupt destructive cycles just as they begin. You already know where that old path goes, so as soon as you identify it, stop and shift to the new way of connecting and honoring each other. Remember the oft-cited definition of *crazy*—doing the same thing repeatedly and expecting something different to happen. Rather than falling into the same familiar trap, catch yourself as soon as your words, tone of voice, and demeanor seem ineffective. Be brave enough to say something like this: "I realize this is not working. Let's try something new. We are creative. We can invent a way to discuss this that unites us. Please talk. I am listening now." You can use the exercises at the end of the chapter to develop more skills to break loose quickly.

Jessica learned to stop a destructive cycle of arguing over the cleaning chores by reframing the scene. "Whenever Bill left the kitchen a big mess, I used to give my usual impassioned speech about cleaning up after himself. I called him a big slob, an inconsiderate, self-centered mess of a person. Now when I feel this energy building in me, I stop myself, step back, leave the room, catch my breath, then enter the room again with a calmer attitude. I will ask Bill what I can do to help and occasionally we will put on some old-time rock and roll music and sing together as we clean up after the delicious dinner he made!"

As we've mentioned, the process of change moves slowly. Be compassionate and patient. A marriage workshop leader handed out a page of relationship agreements to discuss and practice. One participant was shocked to read the first one: "Treat your partner as if he is always right. Accept his point of view as valid and true for him." She commented, "Everything I believed about relationships was challenged by that one statement. My tacit mission had been to change Bob into who I wanted him to be, so we could be happy. If I accepted him as right, would that mean I was wrong? I could not wrap my brain around the notion that each of us is right. To this day, thirty years later, I still have to remind myself of that insight. I am still learning how to listen to, validate, and affirm Bob, so that his way is simply his way, based on his upbringing, mood, needs, experiences, beliefs, and feelings."

Freeing yourself of past baggage and current misbehaviors requires intention, attention, and release of tension. Transforming behaviors you want to modify can be catalyzed with awareness, forgiveness, decision, and action.[3] Like anything else worth attaining, the more you practice replacing unwanted habits with positive patterns, the more you notice the gradual gains you're making toward loving yourself and your spouse.

The next chapter helps you refine the effectiveness of your speaking and listening so that you and your partner can dance through life more gracefully.

TAKING ACTION

Personal Practice: What Is Your Codependency Score?

Rate yourself on a scale of 1 to 5 for each of these main characteristics of codependency, where 1 means the statement does not sound like you and 5 is very typical of you.

_____ I am afraid of being rejected or abandoned. This fear makes it difficult for me to end a relationship, even when I feel very misunderstood or mistreated. As a result, I end up feeling trapped.

_____ I too often try to take care of my loved ones, neglecting my own needs, feelings, and interests.

_____ I tend to feel overly responsible for my partner's feelings and problems.

_____ I tend to either dominate my loved ones or to behave submissively.

_____ I frequently blame or shame my partner.

_____ I am told that I am too controlling and manipulative.

_____ I feel so entangled with my partner that I often take on his or her moods.

_____ I lack clear boundaries and the confidence to assert myself.

The higher your score, the more likely you are to be stuck in restrictive patterns of thinking and behavior that result in codependency. If you attained a score of 24 or more, be gentle and compassionate with yourself. Being aware of your codependency is the first important step in resolving your patterns. Talk with your partner or counselor to design a plan for changing from the old habits to new pathways of thoughts and behavior. Use the 21-Day Challenge below to help you. Receiving support to heal from codependent patterns uplifts all involved.

Personal Practice: 21-Day Challenge

Use your journal to track your progress for twenty-one days.
   Draw this continuum in your journal.

X _____ X

Here I am now   **Where I want to be**

Select one codependency characteristic where you rated yourself a 4 or 5 from the list above. Write this one codependency trait in your own words beneath "Here I am now" on your continuum. Describe in your journal how that trait affects your relationship. Now beneath "Where I want to be," write how you would like to behave instead. Record in your journal how such actions could favorably affect your relationship. For example, "I tend to blame my partner" is where you are now. You might then list, "I want to act more kindly toward my mate" under where you want to be.

Set your intention in clear, detailed words and powerful imagery. For example, visualize your face and body relaxed as you accept responsibility for something that you have previously blamed on your spouse. Describe the small steps you can take to change the behavior or thought pattern. For example:

> *Here I am now:* I am blaming my partner for a bunch of trivial things and she gets annoyed. Then we fight or avoid each other.

> *Where I want to be:* Each time I hear the critical tone in my voice, I can take a deep breath and reword the statement to be neutral or compassionate.

Take twenty-one days to experiment with new ways of thinking and acting.

1. Write your desired behavior on an index card, in the first person, present tense.

2. Read it several times each day.

3. Rehearse it in your mind and in your heart.

4. Remind yourself and refresh your commitment several times daily.

5. Look into your eyes in the mirror and affirm your intention. For example, breathe in, "I am"; breathe out, "kind and patient." "I am kind and patient with my partner."

6. Practice on your own or ask your partner for support and see what she notices.

7. After twenty-one days, talk with your partner about how your interactions are different.

Awareness of your patterns of behavior, rooted in your upbringing, programmed by nature, and influenced by those around you, is helpful in achieving interdependence in your soulful relationship. Learn more from articles, books, counseling, coaching, seminars, retreats, and others' stories.

Soulful Connection: Sentence Completion— If Only My Spouse Would ...

During an in-house date, each of you makes a short list of what you want from your partner to feel more satisfied in the marriage.

Of course, expecting your partner to satisfy all your desires is unrealistic and unfair to him. You might feel that if only he would do what you want, you could relax and enjoy the relationship. Express your specific expectations aloud for greater awareness. You may notice how your past programming affects you in today's relationship. Your unspoken desire to have your spouse respond to each of your wants is one of those pesky blind spots.

Facing each other, decide who will speak first and who will listen first, without responding.

Speaker:

> "If only you would ..., then I would be happy."
>
> "If only you would ..., then I could relax."
>
> "If only you would ..., then I would love you more."

Switch roles.

Share with your partner how you feel and react to what she said. Did some of her statements trigger your hot buttons or past wounds? Be careful not to use this information against each other, especially in a heated argument later. Build trust and intimacy in sharing so vulnerably.

Soulful Connection: Practice Forgiving

As you work through the following exercises, keep in mind that they are intended to be helpful and proactive, not undermining or hurtful. Encourage each other to be honest, patient, and compassionate. You may decide to do these three exercises on separate occasions or in one sitting. If you opt to do them in one sitting, set aside ninety minutes to two hours of uninterrupted time to concentrate. This can be part of an in-house date, with fun to follow.

1. Define forgiveness for yourself and share your ideas and sentiments with your partner. You may not agree with each other. That is fine. Try to find common ground to begin with, so you can learn from each other. You may start by exploring words like *compassion, empathy, understanding, listening, accepting, healing.*

2. Select an initial speaker and listener.

    Speaker: Think of an unresolved issue you have with someone other than your partner. Focus on what you have not forgiven and what you would like to forgive. Scan your body for signs of tension and discomfort.

    Listener: Be sure to pay attention to the content and the emotional tone of your spouse. Do not interrupt or try to fix the situation. Just ask for clarification, if needed.

Speaker:

- Briefly describe the unresolved issue.

- Express the emotions that arise in discussing this issue.

- Focus on an area in which you become stuck and cannot further release your resentment or hurt at this time.

- Try methods with which you are familiar, such as deep breathing, imagery, metaphor, healing touch, praying, stretching, or contemporary energy-clearing therapies,[4] to accelerate your release of resentment or hurt. Realize that you have the choice to let go and to free your energy for more life-giving experiences.

- After you sense some release, scan your body for areas of relaxation and tension. Let go a little more. Notice your heart in the left and center part of your chest. Can you feel more space to breathe? Has your mood become lighter? Let your partner know what you are experiencing.

Listener: Share your observations after the speaker feels at least temporarily finished with these steps.

Switch roles. Then discuss together what you are learning about the process of forgiveness and what you feel you need to practice further.

3. Now start discussing together a mildly upsetting current situation that is lingering between you. In asserting yourself, you are more empowered. Use this simple technique to clear distressing situations before they escalate in intensity: "I feel ... and I need ..."

   Describe the situation briefly, without accusing or blaming. Then express your feelings from your perspective, beginning with "I ..." For example, "When you told me the house was a big mess, I got mad because you did not understand how hard my day has been. I defended myself and yelled at you." Ask your spouse for what you need to ease your discomfort and to feel more connected, such as, "I need you to listen about my awful day—and please give me a hug."

Soulful Connection: Regarding Our Relationship ...

Take thirty to forty minutes on this exercise to clarify what is important in your relationship. This helps to cut through the usual layers of communication so you can attune to your core needs, values, and upcoming decisions.

Find a quiet place at home, outdoors, or at a retreat setting. Take turns as #1 and #2.

Begin with #1 asking #2 each question. The person asking the questions (#1) records the answers to all questions in the summary (last) round.

Precede each question with the phrase, "Regarding our relationship ..." Repeat each question three to five times. Then repeat each question once more, requesting a brief summary or synthesis of the previous responses.

Regarding our relationship ...

... what do you need?

... what do you fear?

... what are you committed to?

... what do you hold dearly?

... what new decisions are you ready to make?

#1 reads the list aloud. Both partners listen carefully to #2's responses.

Switch roles so that #2 now does the asking and #1 replies. Again, record the last round of each question. Read aloud. Thank your partner for sharing.

Discuss what you are learning about what is important for the other person and for yourself. Make a list of your core values, needs, and upcoming decisions.

Display your lists of what is essential in your life and relationship in a prominent place. This reminds you of your core values. Perhaps you want to make it a decorative work of art or craft it into a mission statement.

You can repeat this exercise, adding your own questions or format to serve your particular purposes. Just clear away the usual chatter so that you can get to the crux of your needs and values. Make sure you carry out new decisions with proposed plans of action and follow through by implementing those action plans to build trust and closeness.

Personal Practice: Stop and Shift

Assert your power to take a shortcut to effective action. There is no need to analyze behavior by asking questions like these: "Why am I like this?" or "What's wrong with me?" This kind of pondering is rarely useful. Just stop what does not work and shift to the way you want to be.

Brainstorm what you can do to interrupt your negative or dysfunctional patterns. Select two to three ways to shift your behavior. Experiment. Make a list in your journal of what works for you. When you notice that your thoughts, words, or actions are ineffective, destructive, or hurtful, pick one of the choices from your list of behavior shifts and implement it. This will lead you back to a more soulful way of interacting.

Speaking and Listening in a Dance

Mastering Soulful Communication

When the trust account is high, communication is
easy, instant, and effective.
—Stephen R. Covey, *The 7 Habits of Highly Effective People*

While working at the computer, your spouse calls out, "Honey, what's
for dinner?" You instantly respond, "Did you walk the dog?" Does this
simple scenario sound familiar? Two people are speaking, but no one is
communicating.

Whether it's because you're in a hurry, distracted, or in mindless
mode—we've all been there—you send your messages telegraphically,
with quick to-do's, commands, or information sound bites. Yet when you
communicate with your partner this way, you often miss having in-depth
conversations. It is a fine art to know what to say, when, and how. To listen carefully and kindly is an even more refined skill to master. No wonder that the goal of most couples in counseling and coaching is to resolve
communication difficulties.

One secret of soulful marriages is discerning when quick sound bites are efficient and effective and when they are not. When surface-level talk is detracting from your closeness, you need to actively restore a deeper level of listening and response.

This chapter focuses on becoming aware of what contributes to soulful communication. By being responsible for your own thoughts and self-talk, you can choose new ways of relating to your beloved. As you learn to change old negative patterns, you contribute to the smooth dance of speaking and listening with your partner.

Learning Your Steps

Communicating—the act of speaking and listening—has its own rhythm, its own dance steps. You and your partner each have your own style. Are you dancing together? Is it like a ballet? a tango? a waltz? hip-hop? country swing? Are you always the leader in the dance or are you often the follower? Are you timid and afraid of stepping on your partner's toes or do you gracefully flow and glide together across the dance floor of life?

Recognizing your own personal style means you can understand how your style works with your partner's style. In becoming a soulful couple, you refine your communication styles so that you flow together in a graceful waltz or a sizzling salsa. But first let's start by understanding three basic components of speaking and listening: content, feelings, and context.

Content

In conversation, content is the subject matter—what you talk about, such as what happened to you or to one of your family members or friends, or about something in the news. It's telling a story, filling in facts and details, or making logistical plans. Content describes the who, what, where, when, how, and why of what you want to communicate.

Feelings

Feelings underlie what you are communicating to your partner—the tone of your message. They take us beyond words to provide critical information so we gain full understanding. As a metaphor, think of feelings like a crayon box. The four primary colors are mad, sad, scared, and glad. Expand your color palette and you add disappointed, anxious, excited, curious, hurt, frustrated, lost, and much more. If you speak strictly on a content level, you are conveying only partial information to your partner. Likewise, if you listen solely for content, you are likely missing key information regarding your partner's feelings, which can guide you in making a soulful response.

Context

The context in conversation is the setting or situation in which the communication takes place. It involves the time and topic as well as the physical, social, and emotional settings. The context of a conversation that takes place in a doctor's office is very different from the context of a conversation that takes place at a wedding. Context can also reflect the foundation, core values, and underlying beliefs embedded in the conversation.

Putting It All Together

Learning to listen for and speak in relation to content, feelings, and context is one of the greatest gifts you can give your partner. Practice listening for the content of your partner's sharing and learn to reflect back or inquire about what you are hearing. For example, "You had a doctor's appointment today. What happened?" Listen to the details and ask relevant questions.

Increasing your awareness of your feelings and those of your partner, and being able to name them, will foster deeper communication. When you name and acknowledge a feeling, and give

> Loneliness doesn't come from having no one around you, but from being unable to communicate the things that are important to you.
>
> —Carl Jung, *Memories, Dreams, Reflections*

it space to be expressed, its force dissipates much more easily. If you do not acknowledge the feeling, if you judge it as bad or wrong, or if you stuff it deep inside, then the imprint lasts much longer—as often occurs with trauma, abuse, or heartbreak. By learning to detect and name feelings within yourself and your partner, you promote effective communication. For example, "I know that you had your doctor's appointment today. How are you feeling?" Pause and listen, be empathic, ask for clarification. Find out if support is needed and wanted.

Finally, use your awareness of context to set the tone for or course of the communication. Or, in the midst of an escalating encounter, if effective communication is breaking down, shift the context to help redirect the course of the conversation. Eye contact, physical touch, and hugs can be comforting.

Here are some examples of how to establish positive context for a soulful conversation, even if the topic is volatile:

"Let's spend fifteen to twenty minutes tonight before we go to bed to clear up what happened last night. Then we can both sleep well."

"I need to talk—I am aware of some issues that are stored in my tissues."

"I am so upset right now. I just remembered something that happened when I was our daughter's age. Please listen. Don't judge or fix or try to change me. I need love and healing. If this isn't a good time, when can you give me your undivided attention for a while? Can we walk and talk on Saturday, so that I can clear these emotions? Meanwhile, I am going to write down my memory, thoughts, feelings, and how this has affected me ... and how it affects our relationship."

"I know you're discouraged about your job search. I wonder if taking a class to brush up on some of your skills might make you more marketable. Why don't you find a class, then I'll take a course at the same time so we can attend school together. It could be fun. We can go out for dessert after class. What do you think?"

Speaking and listening in a dance together can open the way to soulful depths that make life meaningful. When couples get out of step with each other, all kinds of breakdowns occur. With increased awareness of the components of soulful communication, you can restore the rhythm.

The Aha Moment: Helen

Helen was suddenly laid off from her long-term job. She and her husband John had to make some quick decisions. Helen soon secured a new position, but it was thousands of miles away. Moving appealed to her for many good reasons. John was in shock and was not thrilled about moving out of state, but reluctantly agreed to join Helen. When it came time to pack and move, Helen took command. Being a go-getter with an assertive personality, she gave John to-do lists while she was at work. He did not complete all of them on her schedule and to her liking by the time she came home. This led to fighting. She was ready to leave without him.

Her anxiety was becoming overwhelming. She needed him to behave as instructed. What Helen didn't realize is that, as a couple, they were acting more like a mother and a son than as two adult partners. This dynamic was draining their energy and adding more stress to the already demanding tasks of packing, selling their home, and relocating to another city. Communicating effectively had taken a backseat and the effects were manifesting in destructive ways.

In our counseling sessions, we discussed ways of restoring healthy communication. Helen began to realize that John has his own style of doing things, and she gradually stopped pushing to control her husband. As she trusted John to get things done, Helen found she had more energy and thus more goodwill toward her husband. They worked together more effectively, communicating what tasks needed to be done and in what order. Cautiously they began dream-building about their new life by the sea. As you may guess, they came through the process valiantly and drove the moving van, as scheduled, onto the open road.

I spoke to Helen after they arrived at their destination and she said the best advice she received from counseling was to love John through all of this. The couple's enthusiasm and joy for making a new life together has deepened their love. Months later, she sent me pictures of their boat and all the fun they were having as a couple in their new life!

Being Responsible for Your Thoughts

As you can see from Helen and John's experience, you have choices in how you deal with small or large stressors in your life. Increasing your awareness of your inner dialogue—how you speak to yourself—helps you communicate with your partner much more consciously and effectively. Are you aware of how you talk to yourself? Most of the time the mind is playing and replaying prerecorded messages. The mental chatter goes on and on. Take a moment to listen in. What do you hear? Are you judging, labeling, comparing, worrying, remembering, wondering, celebrating?

You can begin to have more control over your self-talk by understanding how the mind works. A typical thinking pattern goes something like this: "What I think leads me to how I feel, which leads me to react to what is going on around me, which drives me to act. Then I get feedback that reflects how I think."

The negative loop of thinking-feeling-reacting-acting can trap you if you are not aware of the circular nature of your thinking. To break free from such a destructive cycle, you need to change the thoughts that lead to the outcome, which often involves revising your perspective of a situation.

For example, you judge your husband as a poor housekeeper for not removing the crumbs under the toaster when he cleans up the kitchen. Then you feel angry and talk meanly to him. He reacts by yelling at you. Your evening devolves into a cold war. Now try shifting your thoughts to being grateful for the lovely dinner you just shared and how nice it is that he is cleaning up the kitchen. You thank him, hug him, joke with him about missing the crumbs under the toaster, and have a pleasant evening together. By managing your thoughts in the latter scenario, you cultivate harmony in your relationship.

The simple practice of deep breathing can slow down the mental chatter and allow you to take control of your thoughts. As the speed of your thoughts slows down, you gain awareness of thoughts that preoccupy your mind, and how they affect your feelings and bodily sensations. Learn to calm yourself with slow, deep breathing when you become agitated and wait to speak until you are calm. When you have inner harmony and feel centered, your thoughts tend to be more coherent, your voice clearer, and your words more carefully chosen.

Strengthen your mental muscles by guiding your thoughts back to what is essential to you. You can learn how to center yourself through repetitive practice, like doing reps at the gym. Self-correcting your thoughts, words, and actions is a powerful way to live. During times of fatigue and stress, your mind may fall into old, familiar patterns that have not served you or your partner in the past. The old adage "Don't go to bed mad" may not be the best advice. When you're tired, your conversation may degenerate into accusations and recriminations. You may be much wiser to say good-night with the promise of talking the next day to clear up the problem.

Old ruts of thinking may manifest in your inner self-talk as excessive complaints, unwarranted assumptions, exaggerations, and overgeneralizations. When you detect and choose to sidestep these kinds of mental distortions or traps, you think and speak more genuinely and cogently. When your mastery of your inner communication improves, your outward communication is likely to improve over time as well.

As you become more aware of your thoughts and their effect on your communication, you may need to shift your beliefs from an old, outdated model to a more constructive one.

Shift in Consciousness

Conventional Model: Mindless Communication

Communication is a natural process and requires no training or practice. You just talk and see what happens. If it doesn't go well, just blame the other person.

Soulful Model: Mindful Communication

Effective communication requires positive intention, attentiveness, and gradual refinement. Sometimes pent-up emotions, often not directly related to the topic at hand, emerge in conversations with your partner. You may both be surprised at the intensity of those feelings. By taking time to acknowledge those emotions and their possible sources, you can clear the storehouse of emotions. This will enable you to respond more appropriately to current situations.

Barriers to Constructive Communication

Remember a time when you expressed a feeling, a need, or a request and your lover listened and responded appropriately and in a satisfying way. Breathe in that pleasant memory now. Doesn't that feel great? Do you wish you could bottle this ease in communicating?

Now remember a time when the communication between you two was terrible. Dare to mentally review the disturbing experience as a movie in your mind. Misunderstanding each other can lead to hurt, disappointment, withdrawal, temper flares, verbal abuse, internalizing, and depression. You know the feelings.

A complete list of ways in which communication gets inhibited, derailed, or just plain ugly would fill pages. Rather than overwhelming you with a comprehensive list, here are common patterns of dysfunctional communication. Without feeling guilty, identify which ones characterize your behavior with your spouse. If you want, you could rate yourself on a 1 to 5 scale for each one.

1 _____ 5

Rarely   Very Frequently

- Tuning out: Not paying attention or being present when spoken to; using media to distract you; focusing on what you are going to say next instead of listening

- Interrupting: Completing your spouse's sentences; chiming in with what you want to say before your mate finishes speaking; abruptly changing the subject

- Discounting: Negating, invalidating, undermining, or minimizing your partner's expressed needs or feelings

- Using dismissive terms and nonverbal expressions or gestures, such as saying, "Who cares?" "Whatever," "Yes ... but," eye rolls, hand-flicks, twisting your mouth while shaking your head from side to side

- Monopolizing: Dominating the conversation so that your partner has little opportunity to speak (can't get a word in edgewise)

- Mind-reading: Assuming that you know what your mate is thinking or feeling before she tells you; drawing conclusions before verifying that those were her thoughts or feelings

In addition to these barriers, another major block to soulful communication involves battling for power and control. You may notice that you have a tendency to adopt either a dominant, one-up position in communication or a submissive, one-down posture where you seek to yield control. Perhaps you use a combination of these two styles or flip-flop between them when you're under stress.

One-Up Characteristics	One-Down Characteristics
physically or verbally aggressive	passive, sometimes cowering
dominating, intimidating	submissive, perhaps passive-aggressive, e.g., giving your partner the silent treatment
critical, blaming/shaming	guilty, shameful
grandiose, arrogant, superiority complex	overly humble, inferiority complex
condescending, "holier than thou"	self-deprecating
interrogating, probing	avoidant, minimally responsive
competitive	overly compliant

The most prevalent dynamic among couples entails the seesaw effect of one person attempting to dominate the conversation and the other behaving submissively, then switching roles. For example, you may feel righteous about a position you are taking in a conversation and try to make your partner, who disagrees, concede the point. Your partner resents your manner and either becomes passive-aggressive or switches into the one-up role in an effort to take control. Frustrating struggles lead to a stalemate—round and round the same loops. Dizzy, destabilized, or depressed, you may back away from your partner and at some level give up trying for any kind of meaningful exchange. The energy is stalled and dull.

A more volatile scenario occurs if both of you vie for dominance. The energy heats up, tempers flare, voices escalate. Such battles may be fueled by excessive use of alcohol or drugs. The scene becomes inflammatory, as depicted in the classic movies *War of the Roses* or *Who's Afraid of Virginia Woolf?*

In any of these power plays, when you each strive to hold your ground, the most that is accomplished is a temporary venting of feelings like anger, frustration, or hurt. As the saying goes, "You might win the battle, but you end up losing the war"—that is, you undermine your relationship.

Imagine a big red balloon. As the daily pressures mount, the red balloon fills with complaints, criticisms, cynicism, resentments, and betrayals. The tension keeps building until the balloon finally bursts. The explosion happens, the mess is made, the hurt is inflicted. Then the cleanup happens, maybe even through make-up sex. Without intervention, this filling and emptying pattern continues, with the cycles becoming more predictable and potentially dangerous. Many relationships are destroyed by this exhausting dynamic.

By contrast, if you both act in a one-down manner, meaning you each seek to yield control to the other, you conspire to avoid or minimize conflict. It is equally stressful to continually try to keep the peace. Love is messy. Issues come up; conflict happens. In this passive style, more and more stress is internalized, without permission or the skill to release it. You may feel sick, achy, and tired, your emotions dull and lackluster. You may feel bored or dissatisfied. Are any of these consequences of actual peace?

> We are stronger when we listen, and smarter when we share.
>
> —Queen Rania Al-Abdullah, spoken in an acceptance speech of the YouTube Visionary Award

There is hope. Even though you may be challenged or frustrated, persist in learning ways to resolve conflicts assertively and cooperatively. You can unlearn the patterns of reacting in aggressive (fight) or passive (flight or freeze) ways and approach communication with your spouse in more intentional ways. You can release stress, promote health, and open the way for more soulful expression. When you replace your primitive reactions with conscious responses, you can approach each other by means of clear communication and work things out.

Assertiveness: Respecting Yourself and Your Partner

Fortunately, you can communicate powerfully without engaging in power struggles. The happy medium between aggression and passivity is the arena of assertiveness. Assertive communication involves maintaining your dignity while speaking respectfully to your mate. This mode of communication allows for power with your partner rather than power over your mate. When you reduce your defensiveness, you are more open and genuine in your communication.

Building skills and attitudes for assertive communication can enhance your self-confidence and eliminate useless fighting. Here are some helpful guidelines:

- Be aware of and responsible for your own issues that color or filter how you view your partner. Do your own work so that you can be a soulful vessel of love, compassion, and conscious progress.

- Take responsibility for your messages by using *I* statements: I need ..., I want ..., I feel ..., I request ...

- Use active listening to reflect or paraphrase what you hear your mate expressing, to gain clarity and understanding.

- Check with your partner to ensure that you correctly and sufficiently perceive his message.

- Be as specific and concise as possible; brevity is often powerful. Remember, nobody wants to be lectured.

- Know when and how much to express yourself, as well as when to edit or withhold your remarks.

- As much as possible, substitute the word *and* for *but*. Saying *but* often has the effect of undermining or negating what was previously stated. Your partner is likely to feel defeated when you continually respond with *yes, but* ... Saying *and* affirms all aspects of the thought or feeling.

- Develop personal boundaries: Set limits where necessary or desired. Learn to say no without feeling guilty for doing so.

- Make agreements during calm times, based on your commitments, values, and needs. Follow through with proposed plans and congratulate yourselves for successes.

- Be aware of your flaws, weaknesses, or unhealed aspects of yourself and refrain from using them against each other. Forgive yourself, yet be accountable for your behavior.

By learning to speak for yourself, telling your truth, standing up for what is important to you as well as really listening to your partner express his feelings, needs, and requests, you are likely to find a suitable win-win solution that leaves you both satisfied.

Shift in Consciousness

Conventional Model: Your Partner, the Mind Reader

If my partner really cares about me, she will always know or anticipate what I need; I should not have to ask for my needs to be met. If I have to ask, then my mate does not get credit for supporting me.

Soulful Model: Clarifying Your Thoughts

My partner cannot discern my needs or read my mind in every moment and situation. When I want my spouse to recognize my needs or feelings, I must take responsibility for telling him. I ask for what I need and accept his support gratefully.

One way to help you better understand assertive communication is through the imagery of a cup—a feminine principle—and a sword—a masculine principle.

When you are truly present with yourself and your spouse, you are using the cup energy of receptivity, compassion, and gentle holding, like a mother soothing a baby. When you are able to clarify, decide, direct, and set boundaries, you are using sword energy. Imagine a knight holding his sword overhead, declaring his dominion over his land. Use this power wisely!

This cup energy is supportive, yet in the presence of too much comforting cup energy, you or your partner may become unmotivated, complacent, or lethargic, or perhaps even feel suffocated. Conversely, if the sword dominates the conversation and the relationship, you may feel demeaned, belittled, and disempowered, or, conversely, rebellious, angry, and explosive.

Too much of either principle is unhealthy. It is not either-or; it is *and* that has the power. To balance the cup and sword, you allow the cup energy to hold you and your spouse in respect, honor, and love, *and* use the sword, together with the cup, for potent expression and resolution.

Honoring Your Unique Style and Personality

As you have learned in this chapter, each partner in a relationship has a unique style of receiving and conveying information. As you likely remember from playing the game "telephone" as a kid, what one person says can often be very different from what another person hears. This is true with all modes of communication. You may notice that many communication breakdowns happen because you each perceive a situation differently. The differences are often the result of your primary way of getting information. Do you perceive more mentally, emotionally, or through gut feeling? Take a moment to think about your style of information gathering. Are you oriented more toward

- verbal or nonverbal?
- visual, auditory, kinesthetic, gustatory, or olfactory?
- right brain or left brain?
- needing more safety (roots) or more growth (wings)?
- intense or passionate (fiery), emotional (watery), grounded (earthy), or mental (airy)?
- reactive (emotionally triggered or impulsive) or responsive (clear, clean, honest)?

Now turn your attention to your partner. Pay attention to your own and your mate's patterns of

- eye contact
- posture, body positions
- body contact: frontal, side by side, 90-degree angle
- tone, quality of voice, facial expressions, gestures
- breath patterns
- tempo of speech, movements, and gestures
- emotional tone and mood

By attuning to body language and nonverbal cues, you can learn to match each other's communication styles so that your dance of speaking and listening proceeds more smoothly.[1]

Rating Your Connection with Your Partner

Use this helpful scale to measure progress in connecting with each other.

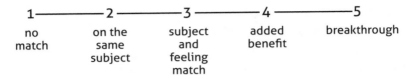

1	2	3	4	5
no match	on the same subject	subject and feeling match	added benefit	breakthrough

1 = Two voices in the air, but missing each other (e.g., "Did I get any mail?" "Where are my golf clubs?")

2 = Both talking about the same subject, but not touching each other's emotions (e.g., ignoring, judging, missing, dismissing, or negating the other's feelings)

3 = Matching the content and feelings of what the other is saying

4 = Talking and listening are in sync with each other, in a beneficial and satisfying way

5 = Sparking synergy, new insights, or depth of realization as soulful communication

When you are discussing a topic with your partner and you both are listening and speaking in harmony with each other, you are at a 3 on the scale. This is a good target to aim for in your conversations. Amazing conversations involve frequent responses at levels 4 and 5; such consistent attunement is rare. Those kinds of conversations are definitely soulful.

Dealing with Stress and Anger

Sometimes communication gets messy. In times of stress and conflict, it is important to know your personal reaction levels so you can determine whether you are in the right frame of mind to contribute to healthy, productive communication.

Check in with your body and breathing right now to determine your level of intensity of emotion or stress. What number would you assign to your state of being right now, where 1 represents a relatively peaceful state and 10 represents a maximum amount of stress reaction or anger?

What are your patterns? In a heated conversation, do you escalate quickly or slowly? Picture steps going upward from calm as 1 to explosive as 10. What is the highest number you can reach and still have control over your thoughts, emotions, and words? Imagine a big stop sign when you get to this number and command yourself to stop and calm down. If you cannot control your emotions past a certain number on the scale, give yourself permission to remove yourself from the conversation to blow off steam in healthy or constructive ways, such as through exercise, raking the yard, cleaning the stove, or hammering some nails.

If you tend to blow up in rage with a temper tantrum at 10, are you and your spouse safe—physically and emotionally? Verbal abuse, name-calling, and threatening are not okay. See the section on "Fair Fighting" below for guidelines on healthy communication. Learn to discharge negative energy with awareness and even humor. A conscious, controlled temper tantrum can be cathartic.

Dealing with anger and high levels of stress may undermine your health as well as your relationship. Engage the support of a coach or mentor to help increase your repertoire of healthy, effective ways to cope with demands in your life. Managing stress and emotions is a sign of maturity.

Fair Fighting: Solve the Problem and Build the Relationship

Skill-building is the name of the game when it comes to clear communication, particularly when disagreements arise. What characteristics do you tend to display when faced with conflict? Do you avoid, escalate, hold on to grudges, or seek to resolve issues? Do you overreact, pile topics together, or bring up one topic at a time? When things heat up, do you give up and want to run, use your anger to intimidate, flare quickly and calm down quickly, or hold in your emotions and blame the other person? Once you have an understanding of your reactions when faced with conflict, you can share your understanding with your partner and develop useful strategies, what is called "fair fighting," to avoid the traps of entangled messes.

The goals of fair fighting are to resolve the conflict *and* strengthen the bond between you and your partner. One without the other is usually not sufficient to ensure a trusting and secure marriage. If you solve the problem but harm the relationship, resentment builds. If you avoid the problem and safeguard the relationship, the issue may keep resurfacing and cause stress between you. Fair fighting strategies defuse intense conflicts and bring more love, light, synergy, and harmony into your relationship.

Your aim should be to develop skills to deescalate and reduce stress so that you can practice constructive conflict resolution. To begin, it is important to be able to identify patterns of an argument that are fair and unfair, proactive and reactive.

Unfair Fighting Tactics

- Overwhelm each other with a long laundry list of grievances.
- Dominate, demean, or intimidate your mate. Attempt to win the dispute at all costs.
- Adopt a rigid position, acting as if your viewpoint is the only right one.
- Call your partner names. Hit below the belt with labels and character assaults.
- Say, "You always ..." and "You never ..."
- Bring up the past and use it against your partner.
- Attack with escalating emotions so that you are both in fight-flight reactive mode.
- Storm out of the room or house and remain out of communication for a prolonged period.
- Impose the silent treatment for hours or days.
- Continue to lash out at your partner for days, weeks, or months.
- Barrage your partner with nasty, sniping remarks and mean tactics.
- Go behind your mate's back to involve other people in your fight or to publicly humiliate him.
- Withhold sex or affection.
- Abuse money, media, pornography, alcohol, drugs.

Fair Fighting Approaches

- Make an agreement to talk when both of you are available.
- Set up a specific time and place; serve food or beverages to provide comfort.

- Choose one subject at a time to address.

- Make an agreement about how much time you plan to talk.

- Take breaks if emotions escalate or you feel that your emotions are getting out of control. You can agree to continue at a specified later date.

- Take turns expressing your feelings, needs, and perceptions of the issue in the form of *I* statements.

- Respectfully and empathically listen and affirm the other's point of view or feelings as valid. Reflect what you hear your partner saying to verify the accuracy of your perception.

- Remember the 1 to 5 scale earlier in this chapter, where the target is a 3. Match the content and the feeling of the speaker.

- Correct any misperceptions or misunderstandings.

- Clarify the problem, rate how intense this issue is for each of you (on a 1 to 10 scale), and brainstorm possible solutions.

- Discuss, compromise, and negotiate as needed. Make accommodations for the person who has the most intense need or concern.

- Design a plan of action with specifics, such as who will do what and by when.

- Follow up to confirm completion. Celebrate! If the agreed-upon actions are not done, rededicate yourselves to completing them. Determine who needs to do what, how, and by when.

Take a piece of paper and write *Unfair Fighting* on the bottom; on the top of the page, write *Fair Fighting*. Fill in the techniques you often use on the appropriate halves of the paper. Then make agreements or guidelines for how to handle unfair fighting issues in intentional ways. Make plans to stop unfair patterns as soon as you recognize them and shift to fair ones.

Post your list of agreements or guidelines in a visible location, such as on your refrigerator or bulletin board, to use for quick reference.

Resolving Conflict: Mike and Judith

We have trouble wrapping our minds around the notion of fair fighting. Fighting comes from our survival brain, which triggers the fight-flight reactions. There is nothing relational about that. Being relational means being self-aware enough to recognize our own wants and needs. We do our best to take care of ourselves before we dump these wants and needs on our partner as his or her responsibility. Only then can we communicate specific needs we would like help with, rather than a vague, "I need to feel safe" or "I need to feel loved."

As a result, one of the things we have found most helpful in resolving conflicts is to stop finger-pointing and name-calling and instead take responsibility for our own contribution to whatever difficulty is occurring. It means we stop telling the other person about himself and instead speak our own truth. If I'm going to tell my truth respectfully, I wait until my partner has finished talking or else we'll have two speakers, no listener, and no resolution to the problem. The more we can come from a place of respect, the better chance we both have of staying in our relational brains and avoiding a clash of survival patterns. Respect is central to or an integral part of love. We both continue working hard to cultivate an attitude of respect. That basic respect allows us to rein in our reactivity, to look deeply into each other's eyes, and to remember what profoundly connects us together for life.

If you feel that the respect for each other has been eroded and conversations do not flow like a graceful dance, seek therapy or guidance, especially for particularly difficult and painful topics. The most common, highly charged areas of tension or conflict among couples include money management, parenting, sexual satisfaction, family of origin, religious or philosophical differences, and addictions. Coping with illness, disability, death, suicide, and other forms of grief may require special professional care, too. Healing is possible and help is always available. Reach out and find what you need for comfort and skill-building.

Celebrate Your Secrets and Cultivate Successes

The quality of your relationship depends on your choices. You can move past the pattern of surface listening, perhaps in a placating "Yes, dear" style, to express love in an ever-expanding listening and conscious speaking style.

The more communication skills you develop, the more choices you have in expressing yourself and in responding to each other. Unlock the secret chambers of your heart. Free yourself to trust. Awaken your soul to be truly intimate, to really know yourself and your beloved. Check in with yourself with questions like these:

- Are you behaving like a friend or a foe?

- Are you trustworthy in honoring your relationship vows?

- Is your partner being your friend or a foe?

- Is your relationship a dance or a battle?

- Are you aware of what isn't working? What should you stop doing in order to shift to a more proactive, effective way of speaking and listening?

Remember to acknowledge what is working in your marriage. Take time to celebrate what is wonderful, lovely, satisfying, and fulfilling. Articulate the secrets of your soulful relationship. Let your partner know how you feel and what you value about him.

TAKING ACTION

Personal Practice: Your Relationship Priorities

Take a few minutes to sit quietly. Breathe with mindful, focused attention. Allow the mind, body, heart, and spirit to come together in this present moment. Open the space inside you to allow the breath to fully rise to the top of the head and to drop down to the tailbone. Let this flow of energy nourish and replenish you.

When you are calm, ask yourself, "What is most important in my relationship with my partner?"

Observe verbal answers, images, memories, or sensations drifting through your mind. Remember times of great joy together. Take notice of what you are feeling.

Name one or two priorities in your relationship. Then contemplate, "Am I acting consistently with what I regard as important in my relationship?" Be a detached witness to your responses without judging yourself.

Try to imagine your soul witnessing you right now. Be aware of what your soul might share with you now about what is important in your relationship, and how to act in harmony with your priorities. The responses may appear as words, images, feelings, sensations, or empty space. Accept whatever is present.

Conclude the exercise by expressing gratitude to yourself for taking time for self-reflection.

You can record your experience in your journal. Share this with your partner, if you want.

If this kind of practice appeals to you, continue it daily for a while. You might engage a spiritual director, a meditation teacher, or a counselor to support you. As the saying goes, "When the pupil is ready, the teacher arrives."

Personal Practice: Clearing the Inner Turmoil

Learn to short-circuit the buildup of emotional reactions to difficult situations. You can use your journal to internally process a concern with this model for resolving conflicts: awareness, forgiveness, decision, action.[2]

Select one situation that is bothering you right now. Ask yourself these questions:

What am I *aware* of in my thoughts? in my feeling heart? in my intuitive gut?

I am aware of _____.

I am wrestling with/confused about _____.

I am holding on to negative emotions (e.g., resentment, bitterness, disappointment, hurt) about _____.

I want to *forgive*, accept, heal from _____.

Once I can at least partially understand and forgive, then I can *decide* to think and behave differently. I am committed to _____ (e.g., being kinder to my mate, expressing my feelings more fully).

I choose to act according to my commitments, so I will _____ (e.g., ask for what I need; be accountable to my mate for my actions).

If you want, share with your sweetheart what you have been working on.

Soulful Connection: Rating Your Communication Barriers

Read the list on page 46 to each other and tell your partner how you rated yourself on each item. Listen to each other compassionately. Be courageous. If you are feeling bold, take a risk. Share how you rate your partner on each item. Do not use this information against each other, but rather to identify the areas you both need to work on to increase the frequency and quality of connecting better. Serve as a mirror for each other so that you can see your blind spots regarding how you block communication.

Soulful Connection: Genuine Attunement and Listening

Take ten to fifteen minutes to share this exercise. Decide who is the speaker and who is the listener.

As the speaker, select a topic of interest to you to share with your partner. The speaker talks about the topic for approximately one minute. While the speaker is talking, the listener engages in a few distracting or annoying behaviors (from the list on page 46 or others) that you sometimes do with your mate. For example, the listener may interrupt to disagree or to make a point, change the subject, roll her eyes, stop paying attention.

After interacting for a few minutes, stop. Take a couple of deep breaths and release the tension of that interaction.

Now have the speaker tell his story again. This time the listener really listens, with focus and interest in the speaker, engaging with appropriate questions or supportive comments.

Switch speaker and listener roles. Do the same exercise with a different topic.

Share the feelings that arose for you during this exercise. Gently accept each other's reactions.

Make a commitment to increase your awareness of these annoying behaviors, stop them once you notice them, and shift to communicating with each other in attentive ways.

Check back with each other in a few days or a week to discuss any improvements that you have noticed. Be sure to be specific in your feedback and requests for more connection.

Be patient! Learning how to express yourself effectively, soulfully, passionately, practically, cooperatively, and proactively requires much practice. Keep growing individually and as partners.

Respecting and Cherishing Your Beloved

The Seeds of Sacred Relationship

Love one another, but make not a bond of love.
Let it rather be a moving sea between the shores of
your souls.
—Kahlil Gibran, *The Prophet*

Respecting and cherishing your beloved is the heart of mature love. Just as the heart is in the center of the body's energy system, this chapter is appropriately placed near the middle of the book. The goal of this chapter is to identify what is at the heart of your relationship. You each have core values that underlie and direct your behaviors. These values, planted deep in your heart, are seeds of potential for love to flower. By respecting and cherishing each other, you nurture the seeds and cultivate your sacred relationship.

Before exploring what it means to sincerely respect and cherish your spouse, let's consider some beliefs and behaviors that accentuate or mask the depth of feeling and positive regard you have for your beloved.

What Strengthens and What Weakens Sacred Relationships

The conventional model of marriage is two halves make a whole; that is, marriage serves to complete each person. You are each incomplete halves who need the other to make one whole: $\frac{1}{2} + \frac{1}{2} = 1$. This is reflected in the common phrases *my better half* and *my other half*.

This traditional model continues to reflect the mind-set of many Americans and still exists in many cultures around the world. In the homemaker stereotype, the woman provides bodily care for her husband and children, prepares food, cleans the house, washes clothes, irons, raises children, decorates the home, emotionally attends to everyone, and sexually satisfies her husband as regularly as he requests. She is the body and heart of the family.

According to the traditional model, the husband, as breadwinner, is the head and brains of the family, taking care of the family's financial needs and making decisions on his own about insurance, mortgages, large purchases, banking, home repair, property maintenance, and retirement. This arrangement has been dubbed the "dollhouse marriage." The body (woman) and the head (man) come together and make one whole unit. During the post–World War II decade, home was regarded as a haven and couples generally adopted these rigid roles without question. You may have been raised in one of these types of homes.

> The purpose of relationship is not to have another who might complete you, but to have another with whom you might share your completeness.
>
> —Neale Donald Walsch, *Conversations with God*

A secret to a strong, soulful marriage—what helps pave the way to genuine respect and cherishing—is to rethink the math of the conventional relationship model. Synergy results when two high-functioning people form a partnership: $1 + 1 = 3$. Partners view each other as complete and whole. You honor the uniqueness of each other and together in partnership you become a new entity of *us*. (For more on this, see chapter 6, "The Power and Beauty of a Balanced Life: Honoring You, Me, and Us.")

In a soulful relationship, you focus on being real with one another, appreciating the best qualities in each other and acknowledging the areas where growth and healing are needed. Roles are fluid. Men may be stay-at-home dads; women may be corporate executives. Access your personal wisdom, passion, and courage to satisfy your needs individually and as a couple and family. You value the uniqueness of each one of you and promote the sanctity of your relationship.

Sometimes you may cling to old values and customs to try to gain some sense of security by embracing the familiar, such as mimicking the dynamics of your parents' relationship. Sorting out what is useful and what is outdated or unrealistic may be challenging.

Shift in Consciousness

Conventional Model: Always Agree with Me

You promised in your wedding vows to always love, honor, and cherish me. If you really love and respect me, you would not get angry with me or disagree with me. You would back me up in any controversy, especially with family and friends.

Soulful Model: Conflict Is Inevitable

Disagreements and upsets are a normal part of all relationships. Your mate may respectfully disagree with you and sometimes become provoked by your flaws, yet continue to cherish you. You strive to constructively resolve conflicts and to honor your agreements.

Unrealistic expectations of yourself and your partner may cause upset and chaos in your relationship. Recall some recent occasions when you behaved in a negative or perhaps even ugly manner. Did your spouse reject you once your dark side surfaced, or did he disapprove of your behavior and continue to accept you? By accepting your human vulnerabilities and occasional acting out, you and your mate lovingly give each other the latitude to express a range of emotions and the space to grow spiritually. Keep encouraging each other to self-correct as soon as possible to minimize emotional damage to each other and your precious bond.

Such acceptance is more easily achieved when empathy and compassion are present, even when you are behaving at your worst. When empathy is not present, you may feel fearful, guilty, constricted, or closed off; intimate connection rarely occurs when one or both partners are on the defensive. You may fight more often, demean one another, call each other names, and miss what is really going on. Your partner may feel that it is very difficult to get close to you, to trust you, to feel safe around you. You may feel rejected.

When such flare-ups happen, the aim is to restore a safe, loving space in your relationship, which will allow your heart's defenses to soften. You may feel as if you're striking a delicate balance between being soft and strong as feelings of vulnerability arise. Knowing that it is normal to go through a range of emotions—that even soulful couples have disagreements—may help you be more accepting of yourself and your beloved.

Love can serve as a poultice that pulls impurities and toxins to the surface. Old behaviors and beliefs surface, even when things are going great. One of you might suddenly say or do something that is hurtful to your mate. Spurts of anger, aggression, or pouty hurt and manipulation might occur. You may be confused or worried that one of you is regressing. "Where did that come from? How did you get that from what I said?" Do not despair. Your reactivity and confusion may allow you to grow into the next stage of soulful love.

Consider the simple, ear-cleaning QTIP. Here is a bit of wisdom to help you detach from the drama: *Quit Taking It Personally*. Step back, breathe, settle down. Use the tools you've learned in previous chapters to deal with your emotions and behaviors. What your partner is going through may have nothing to do with you. Be a conscious observer and a patient lover.

When you are uncertain about what is going on, ask for support, feedback, or clarification in a respectful way. For example, "I can tell that you are upset, but I'm not sure exactly why. When you're ready, please tell me what you're feeling, because I'd like to give you some support." Use your spouse's favorable responses to move communication forward in a positive direction.

Healthy communication, along with the soothing balm of empathy and compassion, helps mend your rifts. Once you find common ground, you can create greater mutual respect. Getting too entangled in your mate's emotional state leads to confusion, resentment, and frustration. Figuring out which feelings and needs belong to you and which can be ascribed to your partner helps clear your thinking. Remember that there are three of you—you, me, and us. Take time to discern the boundaries among the three.

Honoring Boundaries

All relationships have boundaries—individual and shared—built into them. Personal boundaries involve guidelines and limits that you each establish in order to feel emotionally safe or comfortable during interactions together. Common examples of healthy boundary requests include: privacy in the bathroom; knocking on a closed door before entering a room; avoiding yelling from one room to another or intruding in conversations; refraining from opening mail (email or texts) not addressed to you; standing a certain distance apart while conversing; not touching erogenous zones without permission; giving your mate space when she requests quiet personal time.

Like many couples, you may unconsciously harbor resentment or dissatisfaction about how you handle boundaries between you. If you frequently violate your partner's stated boundaries, he is likely to feel disrespected, distrusting, and resentful, which, of course, erodes your relationship. Conversely, your spouse will probably acknowledge and greatly appreciate your consistent efforts to honor his boundaries.

Boundaries are easier to uphold when you understand their roots. Couples often have differing needs expressed by their boundaries and this can stem from differences in their personalities. Extroverts may want contact all day long, while introverts tend to covet time alone to be quiet or do their own thing. Taking the time to acknowledge and appreciate your differences can make respecting boundaries that much more meaningful.

Appreciating Differences

It is a given that you and your spouse are different from each other in many ways, beginning with physical characteristics, skill sets, talents, and personality profiles. Perhaps you come from very different backgrounds, including disparate socioeconomic status, races, regions of origin, religions, or nationalities. One way to look at these differences is that your diversity adds color and dimension to your relationship. That said, your differences can also create additional challenges when you're relating with each other.[1]

One common area of disparity is in personal hobbies and activities. The more passionate your spouse is about her interests, the more likely she is to feel disrespected if you do not validate or at least partially support her chosen activities. A major form of respect, devotion, and validation involves affirming your beloved's main strengths and abilities, as well as core values and expressed life purpose, even if yours are very different. Ideally, you would be able to genuinely appreciate your mate's enthusiasm and to offer strong support for her choices. But realistically, sometimes all you can do is accept or tolerate her interests.

After taking early retirement from his career in education, Bill took up oil painting. He delighted in how his new hobby slowed time down—sometimes he sat for hours in his sunroom working on getting the shading right on just one flower. His wife, Jane, wasn't so thrilled with Bill's new passion. Jane was a high-energy person, and just seeing Bill stationary for such long periods of time drove her crazy. As Bill became more and more engrossed in his solitary work, they spent less and less time together. Jane felt left out, anxious, and alone. One sunny afternoon, when Jane really wanted Bill to get out with her to walk around the lake, she snapped, yelling at Bill about his exclusive, reclusive new hobby. Surprised by her reaction, Bill listened. He had never once considered the effect of his new hobby on her and from her words now, he saw that she felt excluded from something that was clearly important to him. They talked about it. Jane wasn't interested in taking up painting but she thought it might be fun to model for him every once in a while. Bill thought that might be fun, too. Bill also agreed to spend some time each week getting exercise with Jane, her favorite activity. Now they are both happier, healthier, and have new artwork for the walls of their home.

Another example from our couples coaching is this: One partner loves to watch sci-fi movies and the other thinks they are silly. Conversely, one enjoys romantic comedies and the partner thinks they are sappy. They are compromising by each having a night where one chooses the movie to watch together. Another couple found common ground by choosing a director they both admire. They have queued up several of his movies for their cuddle time on the couch.

You and your partner are likely to prefer to give and receive love in different ways. In his widely acclaimed book *The Five Love Languages*, author Gary Chapman cites five styles of loving:

- Physical touch
- Words of affirmation
- Acts of service
- Gifts
- Quality time[2]

The golden rule, "Do unto others as you would like others to do unto you," provides a basic guideline for honoring your beloved. However, this proverb may be confusing when it comes to love languages. "If I treat you as I want to be treated, but this is not your preferred channel for receiving, then you may miss my gift." For example, through coaching, one couple realized their love languages were not being understood by the other. They both felt lonely and irritable in their relationship. Realizing they could share love easily with a few adjustments, they came up with this agreement: Kim's husband says the reassuring words of love she longs to hear and Kim helps him with the yardwork to show her love for him.

Incorporate this slight variation of the golden rule and see what happens: "Treat your beloved as she would like to be treated."

From Gary Chapman's list of love languages or considering other ways of loving, what do you think are the two main ways that your partner prefers to give and receive love? Those ways could be the same or different. Check out your hunches with your spouse. Discussing your styles of loving can be very informative and fruitful, especially to better honor your beloved's specific preferences. It would probably serve you well to have this conversation on several occasions. You are likely to be surprised about what you uncover in your discussion. Keep checking in with each other. Does your sweetheart feel your love? Are you speaking a language that your beloved understands?

The Foundation of Respecting and Cherishing: You

Respecting and cherishing your beloved is directly proportional to your self-esteem; that is, how much you honor and love yourself. The early chapters of this book laid the groundwork for personal development. A secure sense of self is central to the stability and health of your committed relationship. As you gradually develop more of the qualities you desire, such as being present, compassionate, honest, and aware, you have more to offer your partner in any given moment.

How does your level of self-esteem and self-confidence affect your relationship? Take a moment to reflect. Self-love often gets confused with vanity, arrogance, or an inflated ego. But egotism is different than appreciating who you are, savoring life, and honoring your contributions to life. Genuine self-regard is essential and difficult to fake.

Your relationship requires resiliency and flexibility to cope with challenging circumstances and personal upheavals. During difficult times, you may lose some grounding and not feel quite as self-assured as you did during stable or good periods—that is normal. As you shore up your self-esteem, you are likely to observe more calm and contentment in the core of your being. You do not take the bounces as high or plummet as deeply as you did in the past. Think of the metal safety pole that you grab to stabilize yourself as a bus or train starts to move. So, too, you can latch onto the pole of your self-esteem when life throws you around a little or a lot.

Your self-esteem may also be likened to the ocean. The waves on the surface of the ocean may be turbulent, yet quiet prevails under the surface. So it is with your relationship and self-esteem. You can ride the waves of human drama—conflicts with your partner—and continually recommit to being true to yourself—your self-esteem. Do you feel as if the waves are taking you under or are you becoming a good swimmer? You do have a choice.

When you respect your authentic self, you are naturally in a more positive position to honor your partner and the relationship you share. Standing firmly in gratitude, respect, trust, and adoration of yourself and your partner is a great gift. The rare treasure of unconditional love is a secret that makes life worthwhile and meaningful.

Together We Find Focus: Kathryn and Gene

We get somewhat of a surreal feeling when we tell someone we are celebrating our fortieth anniversary this month. When we make the statement, we do so with pride and a sense of wonder. Forty years?! How did that happen? And we don't take the occasion lightly, either. We didn't come by these four decades with ease. Probably no couple who has remained together for a long time does so very easily.

In all, the longevity doesn't account very much for the sense of wonder I mentioned. What is more significant (Gene agrees with this) is that we—our *us-ness*—has survived our individual selves. *We* have outlasted our immaturity, pettiness, quarrels, need to be right, and all the turmoil and divisiveness of the child-rearing years.

We ourselves grew, singly and together. Our polarities don't seem quite so polarized now, as we realize all the more when we care for our grandchildren. Each of us offers a valid, albeit different, perspective. We respect that about each other. Guess we really have mellowed with age. We are friends. We (mostly) communicate. We say, "Thank you" and "I'm sorry" more these days, maybe because we have more time to say those things rather than just thinking them. We try not ending the day being at odds with each other. When things have been difficult, we wake up in the morning and ask each other, "Shall we do this again?" So far, the answer is yes.

Relationship can be like the ocean in its permanence through constant change. Each of us has the same view of that ocean, too, but with a distinct and different lens. We're like a set of binoculars. It takes bringing the two lenses together to find focus.

The Many Flavors of Respect

Like ice cream, respect comes in many flavors, including forms of etiquette, politeness, or chivalry. Do you place importance and meaning on such chivalrous acts as opening doors or do you consider them superficial, outdated, or only for show? Following through on the ice cream analogy, do you regard sincere politeness as generic vanilla or as a more delectable, elegant flavor?

Typically, courtship begins with a lot of mutual attention to proper, best-foot-forward behavior. Although you could remain courteous and chivalrous throughout your relationship, consistent best behavior is likely to diminish as familiarity with one another increases. You could probably identify some ways in which you have taken your partner for granted and acted less considerate over the years. Yet as you and your mate grow more comfortable with and committed to each other, you may also notice a deeper, more expansive respect.

This deep respect reflects your values. For example, if you place a premium on intellect and educational achievement, you would be inclined to respect your spouse's academic prowess. Similarly, if you are career-oriented, artistic or musical, or a fitness fan, you would honor your mate for success in those arenas. More subtly, you could respect a certain personality or character trait in your beloved, such as sensitivity, reliability, or integrity. Do you tell her what you admire? Acknowledging what you adore or appreciate gives love the energy that promotes respect.

Over time, or in momentary glimpses, you can come to recognize and honor your partner's essential nature and gifts. Mature, deep respect can be compared to an aged, vintage wine. As you and your beloved develop a strong, mutual respect, tranquility and harmony tend to suffuse your relationship.

Shift in Consciousness

Conventional Model: Superficial Stereotypes

Men especially value respect and derive their sense of self-worth from feeling respected. Women mainly need to feel special and cherished by their spouses. Validation comes from outside yourself.

Soulful Model: Inner Wisdom

Your sense of dignity is primarily the result of your own self-regard. You, as a man or a woman, strongly desire the special feeling of being respected and cherished by your beloved, yet you do not require others' affirmation to feel worthwhile and whole. Your sense of self comes from your inner wisdom, acceptance of yourself, and striving for unconditional love.

As you develop greater awareness of your own inner thoughts and feelings, you can more readily shift your consciousness to update your beliefs and needs in your current relationship with your mate. You are ever-evolving and changing when you take the path of personal and spiritual growth and transformation.

Tribute to Our Fortieth Anniversary—Celebrating Our Love Story: Jim

My parents' wedding gift to Ruth and me was a Jamaican honeymoon in June 1970. We celebrated our forty-year anniversary in Maui, Hawaii. These absolutely glorious tropical vacations serve as bookends or markers of our tropically warm and radiant marriage.

Standing among lush flowers overlooking the vast ocean expanse at the Garden of Eden Arboretum on the road to Hana in Maui, Ruth and I renewed our commitment to each other. With forty years of history as our witness, our mutual promises flowed like honey. Each of us was beaming and feeling proud of our accomplishment. As therapists who have logged over thirty-five years of relationship counseling, we know better than most that nobody reaches a fortieth wedding anniversary without considerable effort, struggle, patience, perseverance, and acceptance.

We have indeed had to ride many turbulent waves through our marriage, just as we did swimming, boating, and snorkeling in the two tropical oceans of our marital celebrations.

Despite the numerous challenges and periods of emotional pain, Ruth and I can fervently affirm that the depth of love and joy we have shared over these four decades has easily superseded the tough times. Parenting three children and a dog, and now being grandparents, has been incredibly beautiful and meaningful. Given the age range of our children, we have had at least one child living with us for all but six and a half years of those forty married years, so we're actually ready to experience the "empty nest" that many couples dread. What has astounded us is a parallel spiritual journey we've taken through our entire marriage and working together as business partners in a host of projects since 1976—this encompasses 85 percent of our married life.

> It takes no time to fall in love, but it takes you years to know what love is.
>
> —Jason Mraz, *Life Is Wonderful*

The prime spark plug continually igniting and rekindling our relationship has been expressing the range of our dynamic personalities. We've been plenty wild, yet just as sedate; raucously silly, along with deeply philosophical and whimsical. We've been very social and communal, while enjoying plenty of sustained quiet times alone. The list goes on and on. The contrast I most celebrate is our ease and joy in each other's company, yet relishing the occasional weeks we've spent apart on adventures, business trips, family visits, and growth excursions.

Although neither of us believes that marriage is for everyone, our exquisite relationship has been central to our souls' expression and development in this lifetime. I am delighted to declare my love to the woman I cherish above all others—my devoted wife, Ruth.

You may want to develop an occasional ritual to share appreciation of each other. For example, this may be planned, for an anniversary, a vacation, or a retreat, or offered spontaneously as a surprise. Maybe you write a letter to each other, affirm each other face to face, renew your vows (publicly or privately), read poetry, give each other massages, pray or meditate, make love. (See also the "Soulful Connection: Thread of Golden Light Meditation" on page 79.) All these deepen your bond.

As a devoted couple, you can set your course to be soulful—individually and together. This may include finding your spiritual home at a church, synagogue, mosque, Buddhist temple, spiritual center, yoga studio, in nature, or by serving your community. Spontaneous or recited prayer can also be a very enriching form of spiritual experience. How powerful it is to reveal your own wisdom and to affirm your values and ideals.

Spiritual Partnership: Doug and Terry

Author Gary Zukav defines *spiritual partnership* as a partnership between equals for the purpose of spiritual growth. This was the foremost objective we were seeking when we found each other online more than six years ago. For us, it was more important than the classic markers of compatibility, such as money, religion, philosophy, or politics. The cornerstone of our love is respect. Both of us are capable, intelligent adults and we highly value each other's opinions, while respecting the other's decisions and autonomy.

We don't sweat the small stuff, readily giving the other a pass on moods, habits, messes, and quirks. Rather, we prefer to focus on the wonderful things the other brings to the relationship. We look at our partnership as an opportunity to practice kindness, compassion, empathy, and love. We disagree fairly often, but maintain open minds and hearts. Most of our hobbies and interests don't coincide.

We don't do big blowouts on Valentine's Day or anniversaries. Instead, we regularly do little things for each other—share equally in chores and tasks; deliver a perfect cup of coffee bedside on Sunday morning; share our intimate highs and lows.

After six years together, our love has deepened. We start every day with a loving embrace, grateful for the other. We allow each other independence and trust each other. We are best friends.

As spiritual partners, we share a common vision of the highest good, focusing on how we can serve our fellow humans, grow closer to our Source, and create a life of abundance and peace.

Enjoy the process of awakening, as a soulful human, in relationship with another awakening human, who is imbued with a soul. Merging with one another can be lovely. How delicious to join together in ways that encourage, glorify, revere, empower, respect, and cherish each other!

Perspective Is a Choice

Recognize that your perceptions influence your attitudes and feelings toward each other. As a spiritual metaphor, imagine holding a microscope over one eye to see the fine details of your life and a telescope over the other eye to observe the grandeur and magnitude of the universe, of which you are an integral part. Notice that you have choices about your vantage point. If you are overly attentive to details or too critical, you could decide to broaden how you view your life and your partner. If you have too sweeping of a vista and you lack grounding, shift to the microscope lens. Then you can observe more details of your relationship and of your daily life in general. For example, while doing the laundry, you might notice that your husband forgot to remove tissues from his pocket so white lint is all over his clothes. Do you distance yourself from him with judgments and resentments? Or do you chuckle to yourself, picturing how precious he is blowing his nose during the day? Do you separate or join together?

In the December 1992 issue of *Reader's Digest*, Roderick MacFarlane described his grandmother's chosen perspective:

> On her golden wedding anniversary, my grandmother revealed the secret of her long and happy marriage. "On my wedding day, I decided to choose ten of my husband's faults which, for the sake of our marriage, I would overlook," she explained. A guest asked her to name some of the faults. "To tell the truth," she replied, "I never did get around to listing them. But whenever my husband did something that made me hopping mad, I would say to myself, 'Lucky for him that's one of the ten.'"[3]

The gracious and humorous posture that Mr. MacFarlane's grandmother adopted toward her husband illustrates the principle of *wabi sabi* love. This principle is based on the Japanese artistic viewpoint that beauty can be found in imperfection. This lovely attitude involves accepting and overlooking your own and your partner's blemishes, focusing instead on each other's underlying magnificence.

Everyday Ways of Honoring and Adoring Your Beloved

A few years ago, I, Ruth, was visiting my mother at a retirement community in my hometown. We had lunch in the communal dining room with Anna, a former neighbor's mother. I was so happy to see her again after fifty years or so. She was dressed in a lovely skirt suit with pantyhose and heels, earrings, hair styled and eyes aglow. I enjoyed talking with her and my mother, reminiscing about old times and common acquaintances. She said she was now ninety-six. I was amazed. I had to ask her, "What am I looking at? How did you come to be this lovely and lively at your age? You are so beautiful!" She looked directly in my eyes and candidly said in a clear voice, "My husband adored me. He treated me like a queen and always told me how much he loved me. I carry his love in my heart."

Anna certainly was a shining example of how loving and being loved affects your health, your quality of life, and your overall radiance. We can all learn from her and her husband's example of continually respecting and cherishing each other and the lasting effects it can have. What are the everyday ways you cherish your partner?

Honored Guest: Chuck and Leann

Imagine for a moment that someone you greatly admire and adore is coming to visit. How would you greet her? How would you treat her during her stay to make the most of your time together?

At the foundation of our marriage, we strive to treat each other as we would an honored guest. With this in mind, we make sure to take a moment to greet each other after being apart, and to express our happiness in being together again. When we speak to each other, we consistently are aware of the power of our words to hurt or heal.

We cherish each other and we realize that, in the bigger picture, our time together is limited and precious. We also realize that, unlike a guest who visits for the evening, we have committed to a much longer time together.

As we have grown in our relationship, we've come to realize that we're here to help each other grow spiritually. Naturally, in this process issues arise. There is conflict and it can be painful and unpleasant. When conflicts do occur, we've learned to see them as opportunities to bring to light the issues that need work. We do our best to remember this in the heat of the moment and to soften our individual positions so that we can grow. It is not always easy to do so.

Our mistakes and flaws do not define us. Rather, we strive to disregard those things and to see each other's divine essence. We're each willing to visualize the other as being the best she or he can be and we allow each other to be different today than we were yesterday. We envision each other as healed and whole.

As with a guest in our home, we're aware of what an honor it is to be together. We appreciate our time with each other and we recognize the value of the unique role we play for each other. With this mutual support, we each feel cherished and adored—and incredibly grateful.

Have fun with these simple ways to touch your spouse's heart in your daily life:

- Give your partner space to relax, be in solitude, rest, and enjoy downtime, especially in the transition from work to home.

- Honor your partner's request for tone of voice and word choice when speaking to him.

- Surprise your spouse by doing something special; it could be as simple as making the bed and leaving a note on the pillow.

- Complete a chore or two on your spouse's list, like washing the car or folding the laundry.

- Prepare and deliver breakfast in bed.

- Bring home a special gift that is meaningful to your mate, such as flowers or a food treat.

- Arrange a pampering session to massage your lover's feet, head, hands, neck, or back; use your own hands or a handheld massager; try accoutrements such as oil or facial masks.

- Shift the energy in the room: Burn a candle or incense, dim the lighting, put on music.

- Stretch out each other's muscles slowly and carefully, following your spouse's instructions. For example, "I'll lay prone. Please pull my arms back, then take my ankles and pull my feet forward. Let's breathe together. I'll tell you when to stop pulling. Thank you."

- Relieve tension and cultivate pleasure with partner yoga.

- Take your beloved on a ride to a favorite nature location. Take photos, frame them for the top of your dresser or post them on his phone to remember the outing.

- Tell your honey, or write in a letter, what you are grateful to her for.

- Express how much you cherish your sweetheart in your own style, using songs, poems, gifts, or artwork.

- Send texts, emails, or phone messages with sweet flirtations.

- Evoke passion and warmth with sexy talk and gestures to show how attracted you are to him.

- Sincerely compliment or acknowledge your spouse for qualities that you observe and appreciate. Rather than offering global praise, such as "You are so smart and beautiful," say something specific, such as "This dinner was super healthy and tasty" or "Your skin looks so smooth and clear."

- Share silent glances of love and appreciation in the midst of busyness.

- Say, "Thank you."

- Say, "I love you."

- Look into each other's eyes. Smile at each other. Hug, kiss, hold hands.

- Make love more intimately.

- Stop for a few minutes to pray, meditate, or breathe together.

- Hold the other in your heart as a precious, important person; send her loving thoughts throughout the day.

- Design rituals that nourish your soul and elevate your love.

- Take a moment during the day to see, hear, smell, and feel your beloved. Discover the love that is hidden under the pile of to-do's and stressful demands.

- Set up a time and place for a special date to discuss with your partner how you can rededicate yourself to connecting again or more deeply. When you get together, set a time limit. State a few guidelines to make sure you use the date wisely. For example, "Let's spend about thirty to forty minutes taking turns, not interrupting, respecting each other's ideas, and coming to agreement." Take turns describing what would be fun and inspiring to each of you. List agreements about what you will each do, say, or initiate to bring more respect and adoration into your relationship. Follow through.

What would you add to this list?

As you explore the secrets of a soulful marriage, including the power of respecting and cherishing your beloved, you see opportunities for growth around every corner. Honor your partner with kind thoughts in your heart, and share those thoughts in loving words with your mate on a regular basis. When speaking about your partner to your friends and family, be sure to share what you love about him. Holding your beloved in the cup of compassion and using your sword energy, you cut away what you do not appreciate about how you treat your beloved. Take responsibility for your own mental chatter, words, and actions. Cut back on how you react disrespectfully to your mate's behaviors. Sacrifice your own need to be right or in control for the sake of letting love radiate from your heart. Simply by shifting focus from complaint to appreciation, you can elevate your love with humble gratitude.

You are richly rewarded for your ongoing dedication to strengthening and enhancing your relationship. When each of you champions and supports your partner's overall well-being, you flourish as individuals and as a couple. As your mutual reverence and adoration grow, you both are likely to acquire genuine humility and awe—for your marriage and for life in general.

TAKING ACTION

Personal Practice: Being Realistic about Your Partner

Draw this continuum in your journal and record your responses. Notice that your answers may change over time. Focus your mind and contemplate:

1. Where would you honestly place yourself on this continuum?

very critical of my partner ———————————— **idealize my partner**

The critical extreme may reflect frequent or strongly disrespectful thoughts and behavior toward your mate.

2. What negative or unfavorable judgments do you make about your partner?

3. How do you usually convey your judgments to your mate? Remember, you can use the cup and the sword to communicate effectively (see chapter 3).

Conversely, the opposite extreme involves placing your partner on a pedestal or viewing her through rose-colored glasses. Beware of thoughts or comments like, "She is the best ...; the most ...; the perfect ..."

4. What are some ways you deny or minimize your beloved's human flaws?

5. Describe some instances when you have swept things that bother you about your partner under the carpet to try to keep the peace.

6. Define the center point of the continuum, where you feel balanced—not too critical and not too idolizing or, as Goldilocks would say, "Just right."

When the pink cloud of being enthralled with each other dissipates, you may feel that you are not in love anymore. Remember the early days with all the passionate sex and raging hormones? The letdown, disappointment, fear, and hurt of feeling very separate can lead to many misunderstandings. You may simply miss each other once married life is in full swing. Criticism is usually a signal that you are not connecting to each other. Being together in the daily routines tends to knock your mate off your imagined pedestal; overly idealizing does not occur very often, except as a public image to project. Take time to reconnect and experience each other's humanness. If critical thoughts or remarks persist or intensify, your relationship may be in jeopardy. Marriage counseling or coaching is recommended under such circumstances.

Personal Practice: Affirming Strengths and Gifts

Using your journal, list some of the strengths that you bring to your relationship. Affirm the skills that help you regain your balance when life throws you off-center. Describe several of your personality traits or behaviors that you consider as assets to your partner. Acknowledge the spiritual gifts that you offer your partner. Then list his gifts to you.

Take a few deep breaths and settle into your body. Focus attention on your heart. With each breath, deposit loving energy into your heart. Affirm your strengths and gifts. Delight in your spouse's gifts to you. Fill your heart space with glowing radiant energy. Make deposits in your heart often to build your love fortune.

Soulful Connection: Deep Contact

This exercise offers you the opportunity to intimately share your admiration of each other. During your exchange of sincere compliments, be nurtured by expressing your love and taking in your mate's respect for you. Set a date to be with your partner in your home where you will not be disturbed. Turn off the phones and electronic devices. Sit facing each other, making eye contact, and giving each other your full attention.

Take a few deep breaths and gradually relax. Stay awake, alert, and present. Open your heart to receive your partner's love.

With feeling, tell your spouse what you appreciate about him. Offer some specific examples of the qualities and behaviors that you mention. Refrain from making any comments that detract from your compliments, such as pointing out exceptions.

Receive your mate's compliments before responding with what you appreciate about her.

Thank each other for what you shared and express how you feel right now.

Soulful Connection: Thread of Golden Light Meditation

You can use this meditation after the "Soulful Connection: Deep Contact" (above) or as a stand-alone activity. Sit facing your spouse, both with your eyes closed. Take four or five relaxing breaths to quiet your mind. Now, on your next exhale, imagine sending love directly to your partner's heart, as a thread of golden light. As you inhale, receive in your heart the golden light that your partner is transmitting to you.

With each successive inhalation, move the light you are receiving in your heart to the right side of your chest. As you exhale, send the golden light from your right side to your beloved's heart. Giving and receiving this cord of golden light makes a flowing figure eight (a symbol of infinity). Continue this process of sending and receiving for eight to ten breath cycles.

Once you complete this activity, remain seated with your eyes closed for about thirty seconds to sense the immediate effects. Open your eyes and blink a few times to clear your vision. Discuss your experience of this energy exchange with your mate. You could use this exercise to restore loving energy when you and your spouse feel out of touch with each other or to simply deepen your connection. Some couples who are often separated due to work schedules enjoy intuitively doing this practice as a bedtime ritual when they are miles apart.

Personal Practice: Building a Heart Altar

Visualize constructing a magnificent altar in your heart as a judgment-free zone of compassion, respect, and devotion. Picture your partner looking healthy and exhibiting his finest traits. Breathe in how much you admire and love him. Exhale and let love radiate throughout your body. Remember great times that you shared. Bring forth the feelings of love, joy, connection, passion, peace, and having fun. Ah, what a delightful feeling of celebration and gratitude.

You might ask your partner to join you in building a physical altar together. On a small table, windowsill, or dresser, display photos, symbols, quotations, figurines, or mementos from vacations, holidays, or happy memories with family and friends.

Soulful Connection: Exploring Each Other's Faces

This is an intimate and romantic activity to deeply connect with your partner in a special way. Engaging in it may evoke tender emotions.

Position two chairs so that you are facing each other and sitting about a foot apart. Choose who is A and who is B for this practice.

Partner A: Keep your eyes closed and simply experience the sensations and your feelings as Partner B slowly, softly, and thoroughly uses her hands to feel your face for three to five minutes. Avoid any temptation to speak. Afterward, sit silently for a minute or two, then quietly switch roles. Again, both briefly remain silent after Partner A explores Partner B's face.

Then describe your experience, especially sharing the thoughts and emotions that arose while you touched your beloved's face and as you received your partner's touch.

Light Your Fire and Bask in the Warmth

Exploring Sacred Intimacy

> Passion is the quickest to develop and the quickest
> to fade. Intimacy develops more slowly, and
> commitment more gradually still.
>
> —Robert Sternberg, *Cupid's Arrow: The Course of Love through Time*

Remember the excitement of courting, when you felt flutters in your heart and butterflies in your belly in anticipation of seeing each other—or sometimes merely thinking about each other? As long as you could be together, you were often content engaging in ordinary activities. Then, somewhere after marriage (and perhaps kids), you settled into the humdrum routine of daily life. Your romantic feelings may have gradually begun to fade, maybe flickering anew for a special occasion, vacation, or passionate lovemaking, only to dissipate again. Eventually you may become resigned, believing that initial feeling of romance could not be rekindled. You may think, "I am just not in love anymore, or certainly not the way I was."

A secret to cultivating and sustaining a soulful relationship is to reignite the fire through intention, focus, and effort. As you reclaim the beauty of your inner being, you reawaken your desire for intimacy. You are both hungry to be deeply known and to discover more about each other—to be loved and to be free to love. When you consciously shift to behavior that draws you closer to your life partner, you build trust. As you affirm your trust, you let your partner see and know more about you, and intimacy blossoms.

Understanding Obstacles to Intimacy

Intimacy often refers to sexual encounters, but it actually means closeness with another person. While sexual expression can energize and vitalize you and your beloved, that is just one of the many kinds of sacred intimacy that can be expressed in your soulful marriage.

What barriers prevent you from pursuing the intimacy that you desire with your partner? As a human being, you are hardwired to defend yourself against danger, pain, and death. Your primitive, lower self is all about survival. This part of you seeks pleasure and avoids pain. While intimacy is the way you open yourself to pleasure, by its very nature it renders you vulnerable. When you are intimate with another person in a romantic relationship, you may feel a heightened risk of getting emotionally hurt by your mate. In physical or emotional intimacy, you may feel as if you are being overpowered, controlled, or even injured. Having your boundaries violated triggers fight-flight-freeze reactions. You might fight for your freedom, yield to the domination, or dissociate yourself from your mate. If a relationship is not built on trust and security, you may avoid deep intimacy as a survival tactic. You may protect your heart by acting separate, aloof, or autonomous.

Of course, when fear of intimacy is a barrier in your relationship, your personal history comes into play—sometimes in a significant way. Low self-esteem or deep shame may prevent you from showing what you perceive as the unlovable aspects of yourself. Painful experiences in your past may overshadow present experiences so that all you perceive are grudges, hurts, disappointment, and mistrust. The windshield is smudged, so you cannot see your partner or her actions clearly.

Low self-confidence and feelings of unworthiness often engender inner turmoil, anxiety, and depression. These feelings make it difficult to achieve intimacy on many levels, including sexual arousal. You may also experience the push-pull of conflicting drives to merge and separate. Remember the boundaries between you, me, and us—they are certainly at play in achieving satisfying closeness. Love and the intimacy associated with it can be extremely confusing. It is not all neat, pretty, and fun.

Understandably, you may have major barriers to intimacy in response to a history of physical, emotional, or sexual abuse, as well as from physical or emotional abandonment. If you often feel neglected or taken for granted by your spouse, you probably struggle to feel close to him. Shame and self-disdain come from repeated neglect and abuse.

Daily concerns and stresses may also exact a toll, depleting your desire or energy to seek closeness with your partner. Examples of some very common intimacy-robbing stresses are:

Time pressures

Health issues

Excessive workloads

Financial difficulties or worries

Parenting challenges

Family issues

By increasing your awareness of the root of your intimacy issues, and how your defenses sap your energy for intimacy, you can identify ways that you might be sabotaging closeness. Take a few breaths and acknowledge your desire and intention to risk more intimacy; that is a great place to begin.

Opening Pathways to Closeness

To begin on your journey back to fiery closeness, set a time for romance. Show your partner that this is a priority and must be part of your regular schedule. Arrange undisturbed time for cultivating romance. During a date or on a walk, chat with your partner about proactive ways to respark your romance. You might mention ways each of you avoids or perhaps even quashes attempts to get closer. Brainstorm ways to limit or cease those behaviors. Frame this using safe words or gestures to avert an argument and reconnect.

During a quiet moment, ask each other what intimacy means for you. In responding, go beyond previous discussions that you have had with your partner about intimacy. Develop an understanding and acceptance that you each have your own perceptions and needs that may evolve over time.

As you talk about intimacy, you may reveal that sometimes you are frustrated when you reach out to your dear one and he is not available. This may just mean you are out of sync with each other. When one is ready to connect, the other is busy. It may be difficult for both of you to be available at the same moment. In some of those situations, you may feel rejected and conclude that he doesn't love you. Whatever you imagine, it is your choice whether or not you reveal your self-talk to your partner.

The more you let the other in, the more translucent the veils of separation become. Just labeling the disconnect from intimacy can help— "Look how busy we can get and miss each other." You can see the humor in the awkward dance of trying to connect. Devote yourself to building resilience, so that you can take missing each other in stride. Use the longing to connect as a good sign. It takes stamina to run the marathon of your committed relationship. Communication is an important key to unlocking your needs, perceptions, and the pathways to intimacy. Keep talking!

Shift in Consciousness

Conventional Model: Be Who Your Partner Wants You to Be

To be loved, you must be who your sweetheart wants you to be—to consistently accommodate and fulfill your partner's image and expectations. You must cut off or deny the undesirable parts of yourself and only show the acceptable aspects. You need to be perfect to truly be loved.

Soulful Model: Be Your Authentic Self

Healthy relationships allow for each of you to be and act as your authentic self. There is no need to hide the good, bad, or ugly aspects of yourself in shame; you are accepted.

In the conventional model of intimacy, fear and resentment may underlie continual efforts to try to please your spouse and to live up to your perception of her expectations of how you should act in the marriage.

However, in the soulful model, as you feel free to express your genuine needs, wants, and feelings, your energy can flow smoothly. Intimacy builds naturally and you are more likely to feel fulfilled.

Shift in Consciousness

Conventional Model: Playing by the Rules

Roles, rules, and behavior patterns are rigid. Many discussion topics are considered taboo or off-limits. Blind spots are tacitly protected. Keep your relationship constrictive and restrictive so you can be safe. Don't take many risks, so the wild life force does not flow freely. It is worth playing it safe, even though your energy may be less vibrant.

Soulful Model: Bending the Rules

As a couple you mutually create your own guidelines and agreements, which remain fluid, subject to change as needed or desired. No topic is off-limits, and you are willing to risk sharing your inner secrets. You are willing to stretch your comfort zones to get to know each other more intimately.

The soulful model reflects the breadth, depth, and vitality of your relationship. Soulful relating creates space for both of you to express what you need and want in all areas of your relationship. The pathways of intimacy are continually opening, making more room for you to live expansively. When your intimacy is authentic, the stream of giving and receiving seems endless. Who is leading and who is following? Who is giving and who is receiving? Who is stronger and who is softer? The answers to these questions are inconsequential. Love is happening, in all its glory.

You can allow life to bring some unexpected turns of events that give your life new meaning and dimension. Living in the mystery of life can be so invigorating. Let yourself be curious about what adventure is around the next bend.

Staying Clear and Current: Lloyd and Deborah

Having reunited after our strong friendship thirty years ago, we have now been married a year and a half. Together we have discovered these secrets about how to share and deepen intimacy from a place of full permission to live with open hearts.

We are friends, foremost and always.

As best friends, all quirks and foibles are forgiven and even celebrated in the unique soul we love. We are endlessly entertained.

We enjoy the ever-changing emotional landscape without judgment.

We are curious about what will happen next.

We remember that this moment is precious. Our experience is the only one like it. Our beloved is more valuable than any circumstance.

Our partnership is a miracle in motion. We dance with it.

Though we are living the wisdom and maturity of our sixties, our spirits are still as fresh as they were in our twenties. So we bring an everything-is-new attitude to our time together. Here is what we *embrace*:

> **E**ase and simplicity are guideposts.
>
> **M**y healing and freedom are as important as yours.
>
> **B**eing with my best friend is the best!
>
> **R**elaxation is the key. It is often just one breath away.
>
> **A**lways remember our deep bond.
>
> **C**uriosity is the cure.
>
> **E**verything offers a reason to open our hearts!

We *embrace* ourselves and each other, exactly who and how we are. Our simplest and most effective way of keeping things perfectly clear is by asking each other often, "Is there anything you'd like to ask me or tell me?" There always is.

Ways to Experience and Express Intimacy

Just as you and your spouse may have different love languages, you each are likely to have different comfort levels, preferences, and desires for connecting in intimate ways. As a couple, you can continually discover ways to enjoy being intimate physically, emotionally, intellectually, playfully, and spiritually. By accepting your own and your partner's choices regarding how, when, where, and how often you become intimate, you grow more flexible and inclusive in how you define what constitutes an intimate experience. Here are some examples of options:

Type of engagement: face to face, side by side, group involvement

Nature of the activity, such as intellectual or emotional discussion, recreation, adventure

Location: room in your house, outdoors, restaurant, movie theater, foreign country

Cost: ranging from free to very expensive

Frequency and duration of the activity in which you engage

Risk tolerance: the extent to which you and your mate are willing to stretch your comfort zones

Experiment and be creative with your intimacy. Simple things like calling your beloved by affectionate pet names can be endearing. Do you recognize your shared couple-speak vocabulary words or references that are exclusively yours? Do you laugh at your private in-jokes? Do you have funny games you play with each other? Tender moments, shared glances, favorite stories, and memories can be intimate exchanges that bring your hearts closer.

Romance: Beth and Paul

It has been helpful to let go of the *shoulds* and expectations of what romance is supposed to look like. Once we are free from expectations, we can enjoy our unique and daily expressions of love. In the sacred moments of the ordinary, we bring joy to our hearts:

Spooning during the last moments before falling asleep

Smiling as a steaming cup of coffee is delivered bedside

Laughing together—most often at our ever-present displays of humanity, e.g., searching for cell phones, keys, and glasses; using the wrong toothbrush; finishing each other's sentences

Touches, smiles, and looks

Cooking, gardening, entertaining

Playing with our grandson

We love the romantic touches, such as flowers, special dinners, and weekends away. However, it is mainly the daily honoring, encouraging, and joking that nurtures our souls and fills our hearts with gratitude.

To help you savor the small, ordinary moments in life, take some time with your partner to share what you really enjoy.

Enlivening Romance without Leaving Home

Carving out time each week to be together as a couple in special ways can enhance intimacy. Weekly dates, without distractions, also provide stability and structure so you feel more consistently connected. You can share time doing things you enjoy, experimenting with new activities, or exploring and heightening sensual, sexual pleasure. Perhaps your work schedule lends itself to using daylight hours to have your dates. Whatever time period you mutually select, honor the dedicated time together as something you can both count on. This builds trust, cultivates feelings of self-worth, and can bring indescribable joy.

One inexpensive way to spend time together is through what we call in-house dates, which can take many forms. You could simply cuddle on the couch and watch a movie. Kissing, hugging, massaging, making out, and making love can delight your senses and bring you closer. Maybe you are game-players and want to challenge each other to a tournament of cards, dominoes, chess, Chinese checkers, Scrabble, Xbox, or Wii. Together, you may want to cook a special meal, work out, practice yoga, meditate, read or listen to a book, learn a new skill, play music, or create art projects. Organizing your closets or redecorating a room can be very gratifying. Use your imagination to come up with fun ways to be together in your home, without spending any money.

A change of pace can awaken you out of the trance of everyday routine. For your special time together, dress in something exotic or evocative. Light candles or dim the lighting. Prepare a plate of finger foods that arouse the senses. Set the mood to suit your activity. Be creative. Take a risk. Avoid the rut of marital boredom.

Massaging each other with oil or lotion can be relaxing and affirming of your love through touch. Just soothing the hands, feet, or neck can work wonders in de-stressing your mind and body. Sensual stroking and sexual play may evolve from your being together. Allow the waves of excitation and relaxation to take you on a delightful journey into intimacy.

Sometimes keeping the massage and touching purely sensual and not sexual can relieve some pressure or expectations, and set the stage for you to rest deeply. You might want to clarify what you want ahead of time to avoid any misunderstandings.

As a couple, you can invent all sorts of ways to foster closeness. An in-house date may involve a discussion on ways to bring efficiency and effectiveness to your household. Put out a platter of munchies with some drinks. Relax and enjoy your snacks as you design smooth and easy ways to organize and manage the daily flow of living together. Take notes and decide on each person's roles and responsibilities. When you keep your hearts and minds open, you can actually have fun making plans and financial decisions. Congratulate each other and celebrate how well you are working and playing together. Be sure to check back in a few weeks to make modifications, as needed. Remember to honor and respect each other's point of view and needs. Follow through on your commitments to build a strong and trusting relationship.

Envisioning and dream-building allow your ideals to be expressed and energized. An in-house date may involve expanding your imagination together. Share with each other your deepest desires. Get juicy and bold. Together you can brainstorm outrageous possibilities of how your life can evolve. Cut out pictures or search the Internet together, find places you want to live, think of role models whose lifestyles inspire you. The magic is that at any moment you can call forth the qualities you yearn for and sharing those qualities can create a deeply intimate connection with your partner.

Consider playing a game of positive possibilities: "What if ...?" Agree on a theme to brainstorm outside-of-the-box ideas. For example, What if ...

... time and money were not an issue? How would you spend your time?

... you could live wherever you wanted? Which places would you choose?

... you had endless time and means to serve those in need? Who would you help? How would you do that? And where would that be?

Arranging outings requires planning, which can itself be an intimate and rewarding activity. You could follow this process on one of your in-house dates:

Make a list of possible dates you would enjoy out on the town or out of town.

Save the list in an accessible place, so you can find it when you need fresh ideas.

Look in the newspaper or online for upcoming plays, concerts, shows, or expos that you would look forward to attending.

Mark your calendars with your selected events.

Decide who is planning an outing for which month.

Encourage each other to stay committed and follow through with your plans.

Agree to manage your energy during the day of your special event, so that you have plenty left for your date.

Taking It Out on the Town

As you know, there are countless possibilities of where you can go on dates. Making a loving and intentional commitment to a monthly outing promises a fresh venue in which to express yourselves and your love for each other, and gives each of you something to look forward to. You can decide each month who plans and organizes the dates. Simply alternating months can help you avoid power struggles, guilt, or resentment.

Dinner and movies are fun, but they are not the most inspiring activities. Think about that couple you no doubt have seen sitting in a restaurant, staring straight ahead, with nothing to say to each other. Perhaps you want to venture out of your comfort zone and try something new, something challenging. Ice skating, bowling, theater, concerts, nightclubs, sporting events, dancing, yoga or fitness classes, and educational seminars are just a few ideas that can stimulate togetherness.

Dressing up in fancy outfits for a night on the town can be a refreshing break from the everyday and can rekindle that first-glance feeling of new romance. Look like the spectacular king and queen that you are! This reminds you how special you are to each other.

For a creative twist, go shopping for elegant, flattering outfits as one of your dates, in preparation for an upcoming extraordinary event, such as a wedding, a company dinner, or a holiday party. Add some exhilaration to the outing by shopping for silky and sexy nightwear, in anticipation of a bedroom date.

The element of surprise can add enticing spice to your relationship. Surprising your partner with an overnight stay at a bed-and-breakfast, a spa, or a ski lodge can be a welcome respite from your busy lives. Have you tried a treasure hunt with clues leading to a gift or to the bedroom? If you both enjoy surprises, you could take turns arranging a scheduled or spontaneous surprise, perhaps on a monthly basis. What comes to mind as exciting ways to surprise your sweetheart?

Ruth's Wild Surprise: Jim

One late-winter evening in the mid-1990s, I was preparing to spend some quiet time with Ruth at home, when she beckoned me into the bedroom. Ruth told me to sit on the bed and get ready to be surprised. She proceeded to place a blindfold over my eyes and dressed me in what I sensed was strange garb. My curiosity was definitely aroused! Ruth then gingerly escorted me downstairs and into our car, still blindfolded. After about fifteen minutes, I inquired as to how far we'd be going. Ruth simply replied that I should allow myself to experience the full surprise. About an hour later, we arrived at our destination. When my wife took off my blindfold, I was amazed to be standing amid a crowd of revelers inside a large airplane hangar in another city. We were suddenly participating in a masquerade party, with Ruth in a belly-dance costume and me dressed as a sultan. As we partied on, I was delighted to be joined by a harem of five women, including Ruth. I enjoyed the playful, harmless flirtation that ensued. What I had thought would be a low-key, kick-back night at home turned into a colorful, spicy night out on the town!

Whether you are on in-house or out-of-the-house dates, the secret to soulful intimacy is to enjoy each other. During these dates, declare a moratorium on any unresolved issues that may be lingering between you. Schedule another time to work out your issues, a time when you can be proactive and mature about handling the emotional upset, misunderstanding, or hurt. Savor your dates by enjoying each other's presence. You want to be open and available on your dates.

Sacred Lovemaking

Sex is a perennial hot topic in our culture. Discussion about it abounds in the media and in everyday conversation. Do you talk about sex with your partner or is it just something that happens under the covers in the dark?

Shift in Consciousness

Conventional Model: Leading and Following

Men take the lead in lovemaking; women are available and compliant. Sex can be used to manipulate your mate by withholding affection if you disapprove of something he has done. You reward desired behavior by making love.

Soulful Model: Sharing Sacred Expression

Intimate connection with your mate is a portal to the Divine. By being heart-centered during sex, you become more open to spiritual connection. Sex is an expression of love and passion, rather than a means of reinforcing your partner's behavior. Also, rules dissolve: Good girls can be bad; bad boys can be good.

Intimate connection and sexual pleasure are heightened by focusing at least as much attention on pleasing your partner as on receiving personal gratification during lovemaking. An ancient Chinese tale illuminates this ideal. As the story goes, a delicious array of healthy foods is elegantly arranged on a large banquet table. There is a colorful assortment of delectable fruits and vegetables, meats, fish, grains, and desserts, but the people around the table are displeased. They are grumbling, listless, withdrawn, sad, crying, or yelling. They each have been issued a twelve-foot-long pair of chopsticks, which will not permit them to get food into their mouths. Famished and frustrated, these people suffer. Their plight represents hell.

As the story goes on, there is another lush banquet table with the same display of tempting food. The people around the banquet table are smiling, laughing, singing, hugging, and enjoying themselves immensely. They each have also been given twelve-foot-long chopsticks, but they are happy because they have figured out how to feed each other. This scenario depicts heaven.

During sex with your spouse, does your bedroom typically reflect heaven or hell?

Sacred intimacy isn't always and only about the physical act of sex. Sensuality can offer a heavenly way to erotically nourish each other. Being relaxed and sensual can be a delightful prelude to, enhancement of, or substitute for sexual intercourse. There can be great pleasure, joy, and deepening connection in protracted foreplay. Perhaps you tease each other for days, titillating each other with words, stroking, flirting, and provocative gestures. As you brush your teeth in the morning, you spoon against the sink. A playful attitude can make magic happen.

> Great spiritual teachers throughout the ages have stated that orgasm is the closest some people come to a spiritual experience because of the momentary loss of self. With spiritual sex, you move beyond orgasm into a connection with yourself, your partner, and the divine—recognizing them all as one.
>
> —Alexandra Katehakis,
> *Erotic Intelligence*

Sensuality allows the energy to build, to stir your hunger and readiness by delaying or withholding intercourse. Massage and sensual touching without sexual play can help relax you and prepare the way for another time when lovemaking feels right. You could experiment with re-creating your dating days, when you may not have made love right away. You can start making love slowly and sensually as you enjoy exploring each other. Remember the thrill when you first held hands, hugged, or kissed? Sometimes reining in your sexual urges resets the hot button back to the beginning of your relationship.

In all stages of sacred intimacy, clear communication is a vital element in satisfying lovemaking. Telling your lover honestly what is going on with you, instead of just avoiding or rejecting your partner, prevents miscommunication. Be true to your own rhythm and be honest about your needs, feelings, and sexual desires. This helps you build trust and deepen intimacy. It is fine to tell your lover, "I need more time," or "I am too stressed; let me unwind first," or "Let's be sensual, not sexual yet," or "Let's have a sexy date Friday night."

Restoring innocence and piquing curiosity is like opening the windows and doors to let in fresh air. Allow yourself to continually discover new aspects of yourself and your beloved.

Rhythms and Styles of Your Lovemaking

After many years together, it is easy to get lost in predictable sexual routines, which you follow like a choreographed dance. Play with these variations and explore your own:

Free-flowing, playful, fun sex

Endless weekend in bed or vacation sex

Make-up sex (emotionally healing)

Romantic, tender lovemaking

Experimentation with new positions, props, products, videos, books

Deep or mystical ecstasy using sacred Tantric practices

Passion-filled "quickies"

Middle-of-the-night surprise sex

Cuddling, then making out, then sex

Oral pleasuring and massage

Role-playing or storytelling as other characters

Varying the ways you make love can keep you and your partner interested and engaged. Cherishing and adoring each other in the process enriches the whole experience.

Just as you can choose to stop unhealthy behaviors and shift to more effective ways of relating, so too can you open your heart and summon passion. Breathe the vibrant, electric energy through your whole body. Let your passions flow like a hot river through your blood. Lighting your erotic fire evokes your desire and hunger. Can you feel the energy of wanting, pursuing, and arousing your lover? Communicate with your sweetheart what you prefer and need.

Create Your Sensual Setting

To enhance your experience, create a sanctuary for your sacred union. Transform your bedroom or special space into a lush, sensual paradise. Turn off all electronic devices and phones. Remove all distractions. Focus on each other and be present.

Heighten your pleasure by stimulating all the senses. Some suggestions include:

Don evocative apparel, arrange artistic displays, and illuminate the room with subtle lighting or candlelight.

Play music or listen to nature sounds to calm the mind.

Create a scented setting with aromatic candles, incense, essential oils, flowers.

Nibble on sensual, colorful foods; feed each other delicately; feast on edibles on each other's bodies.

Rub oil or lotion all over each other's skin, using a variety of light to deep teasing touches.

Shower or bathe together as you pamper each other and deeply relax.

Allow sexual energy and desire to build, varying the tempo of going slowly and quickly.

Ride the waves of excitation and relaxation.

Use pleasure toys, lubricants, or scarves.

Call each other pet names that arouse your sexual appetite.

Dance or do partner-yoga poses.

Role-play as exotic characters in fantasy scenes.

Be totally nonverbal; only use sounds.

Blindfold each other so your other senses are heightened.

Move from room to room or try new places that have not been blessed with your love yet.

The Soul of Our Marriage: Dan and Elizabeth

Elizabeth and I aspire to a soulful marriage every day. We prioritize our marriage so that we remember not to take our relationship or each other for granted. We make an effort to be self-aware so as to be more present and available to the other. While this is not always an easy task, it is an honest one of self-reflection and self-discovery.

Over the past decade, Elizabeth and I separately immersed ourselves in a wide range of course study in personal communication and sacred sexuality. We incorporate our learning in our conversations, which results in the most open, honest, and clear communication either of us has ever experienced. It allows us to explore our relationship with greater passion. Our verbal and intimate intercourse can last for hours. The depth of our connection on the spiritual and sexual level continues to enrich each of us.

> As a nation, we are in a sexual famine. Simply put, not enough people are getting down on a daily, weekly, or even monthly basis. We're not having sex anymore, and we're not doing things that bring us vitality and joy of life.
>
> —Mehmet Oz, MD, www.doctoroz.com

It is often said that knowledge is power, and that is truly the case in our marriage. With the knowledge we have to foster open and honest communication, we are able to share everything: desires, fantasies, fears, and more. We hold each other accountable to speak our desires, believing that this accountability offers each of us freedom. We have also developed a program designed to educate people in some vital love-based courses that aren't taught in school.

This is the soul of our marriage, which we continually attend to, so that we thrive.

Facing the Shadow of Sexuality

As beautiful and exciting as sexuality can be, it has also been a common source of intense emotional pain, even in loving relationships. If you have not experienced some form of upset concerning sex or lovemaking, you are in the distinct minority.

Recounting and describing the numerous types of sexual disturbances and disorders is beyond the scope of this book. If you continually encounter difficulties and discouragement as a result of sexual relations with your partner, schedule an appointment with a certified sex therapist, a licensed mental health professional, a healer, or a medical doctor. The vast majority of sex issues are psychologically based and have remedies.

Most sexual disturbances are triggered by some combination of these attitudes, feelings, and experiences:

Believing that sexuality is sinful, dirty, or evil

Focusing on sex as a performance, rather than allowing it to be a spontaneous, flowing expression of love and passion

Unrealistic or inflated expectations of how lovemaking should transpire

Excessive concern about appearance and/or size of body parts

Feeling emotionally disconnected from or resentful toward your mate

Feeling neglected or rejected by your partner—in or out of bed

Deception, betrayal, or secret affairs

A disparity between you and your beloved regarding give and take, frequency, and/or mode of lovemaking

Past sexual or physical abuse or trauma

Sexual addiction, including obsession with pornography

Anxiety or depression

Substance abuse or pharmaceutical side effects

Gender or sexual-orientation confusion

Direct, honest, and empathic discussions with your spouse about your feelings, needs, wants, and requests may eventually resolve your issues. Typically, women want to resolve conflicts with their partners before having sex. Men tend to prefer engaging in sex before talking through issues or as a substitute for emotional engagement. It may be helpful to work through these kinds of issues with a professional counselor.

Extramarital affairs or emotional attachments to others reflect a complex web of issues that usually have to do with what is missing in your primary relationship. With proper guidance, you may be able to heal from the deep betrayal and actually improve your marriage. Again, seek some form of professional counseling or spiritual direction for persistent concerns or painful distress. Some couples agree to have other sexual partners in an open marriage or a polyamorous arrangement. This is a very personal matter. Have some candid discussions to understand each other's motives, needs, and feelings before reaching a decision about including other lovers or ending the marriage over infidelity.

Sacred Intimacy, Soulful Love

When you dedicate yourselves to learning and growing, you can enjoy a new level of marital intimacy. As each of you becomes more open to love and spiritual awakening, you provide space to heal personality or ego wounds and express your soulful nature. Love is a holy crucible that helps you burn up the old residue from past patterns and free your energy to be true to yourself. Any defensive overreactions are gradually replaced with proactive responses. Your communication becomes more honest. You celebrate your life, rather than grumbling about it. You honor your soul and the soul of your partner. Are you beginning to recognize that you have come together in this life to consciously fulfill your purpose?

Giving the Big Love center stage in your life story allows you to relax so you can enjoy more lush intimacy and warmth. Welcome Love as a frequent guest in your home to rekindle the flames in your hearts.

TAKING ACTION

Personal Practice: Blocks to Intimacy

Take a few minutes to reflect on and write down your blocks to intimacy. Realizing that everyone has some barriers to being close, identify several ways that you typically guard against love. To get started, complete the following sentences:

What really scares me about being intimate with my sweetheart is ...

If I expose my vulnerability, my partner might ...

I would feel more comfortable or safer if ...

One of my main defensive strategies is ...

Soulful Connection: Acknowledging and Requesting

Affirm each other for ways that you observe one another being your true or natural selves.

Try some of these sentences or create your own:

I admire the courage it takes to show me your ...

I like your genuine ...

I appreciate that you affirm me for ...

Then tactfully, not critically, offer some requests for more permission or freedom to be yourself. Refrain from presenting a list of complaints. Doing so is counterproductive—you sound like a victim and your mate is likely to become defensive and hurt. Try the following prompts:

Please accept my ...

I really want to be able to express ...

When I feel strongly, I want to be able to ...

Soulful Connection: Sensory Awareness

To foster intimacy, it is important to take time to stay clear and current with your partner by tuning in to each other nonverbally.

Sit opposite your partner, with your knees touching. For each item below, take at least thirty seconds to connect nonverbally with your lover. Refrain from speaking during this practice.

Look into each other's eyes.

Observe each other's facial characteristics and smiles.

Hold, caress, or explore each other's hands.

Attune to one another's hearts.

Feel electricity or tingling in your genitals.

What other nonverbal connections can you add to this list?

Afterward, sit apart from each other for at least a minute to examine your reactions to this exercise. Then discuss your experiences. Any surprises? Do you feel more relaxed and stimulated? Sometimes getting away from our normal way of communicating with words can bring richness on a visceral or sensory level. When you don't speak, the senses can awaken and you may have more awareness of subtle energy sensations.

Soulful Connection: Expressing Your Interests and Desires

One partner at a time addresses the following items, while the other listens fully and nondefensively. Practice being receptive to your mate's words, nonverbal cues, and emotional tone. Open your listening so your partner can speak freely. Breathe and relax. Notice any stress reactions and calm down.

1. List five to seven favorite ways that you enjoy relating with your beloved. Describe these ways in detail to help your lover know you better. For example, "I enjoy when we [kiss, hold hands, make love, play tennis, discuss current events, prepare a gourmet meal together, expand our repertoire of sexual expression, attend live theater, act silly]."

2. Make three to five specific requests of your sweetheart regarding how you want her to better accommodate your interests and ways of connecting. For instance, "I have a few requests for you to consider. I would like us to make love on the weekends. I want you to play tennis with me at least twice a month. Let's follow the media more closely, so we are knowledgeable about current events. Are you willing to experiment with new sexual practices? I want to purchase season tickets to the theater and I'd like you to attend with me."

3. Ask your partner which of your requests she is willing to accept, which ones she won't accept, and what modifications of those specific requests your partner proposes. Your partner replies, "I am thrilled that you want to be bed partners on the weekend! I'm willing to play tennis on warm weekend mornings and to watch the news more often, but I don't want to have long discussions about current events. I'm not ready to extend our sexual activity. I can check into the theater packages and let you know by next weekend."

Switch roles so that the initial listener now responds to each of the items: 1, 2, and 3.

Use your fair fighting strategies (chapter 3) to discuss difficult topics that may surface.

Be sure to make plans and follow through with what you agree to do.

Personal Practice: Building Passion

Sexual pleasure can be expanded to a spiritual experience. This is a simple, yet potentially profound exercise that incorporates spirituality into lovemaking.

Visualize this as a meditation. Take some deep breaths, relax your body, and quiet your mind. Tune in to the following words:

> "Behold the two of you, each precious and unique, delicately merging with each other's sweet hearts. Your sense of separateness momentarily dissolves. The flame inside your groin and heart illuminates the path for love to grow and expand without limit. Your hearts become the doorway to the Infinite. Immerse yourself in the Big Love."

After you complete the meditation and feel your own boundaries again, capture the image in your journal, artwork, or poetry, or by talking with your partner.

The Power and Beauty of a Balanced Life

Honoring You, Me, and Us

Be aware of wonder. Live a balanced life—learn
some and think some and draw and paint and sing
and dance and play and work every day some.
— Robert Fulghum, *All I Really Need to Know I Learned in
Kindergarten*

Your intimate life with your partner can be a buffer against the harshness and difficulties of everyday life because, as we all know, life can be overly demanding. The stresses from work, home, family, finances, and world issues can mount and create turbulence in what you would like to be your safe haven. As an antidote to this cyclone effect, strive to achieve balance in your individual life and in your life together as a couple.

By strengthening the intention and discipline to live a balanced life, you allow a colorful, rich life of deep fulfillment to unfold. Some secret ingredients for achieving balance are focusing on spiritual practices, household management, community service, hobbies, and special celebrations that enhance your life as individuals and as a partnership. Also, taking time to clear your mind, relax your body, and restore your soul—slowing down internally and creating inner harmony and centeredness—can serve you and your soulful marriage well.

Balance Requires Mastery over Stress

Just as you cannot devour every delicacy at a smorgasbord, you cannot consistently gobble up all life's offerings. You need time to digest experiences and effectively manage your personal resources, such as energy, emotions, time, space, and money. The pursuit of balance involves recognizing that you are a multidimensional person who values nurturing the various areas of your life. By increasing your awareness of your best inner and outer qualities, you can discern what areas of your life need recalibrating in order to achieve balance.

When life comes on hard and fast, you may feel as though you do not have time to catch your breath—everyone wants a piece of you. Stress has been aptly defined as a condition in which the demand seems greater than the resources you have to deal with the situation. For example, it may seem as though your to-do list exceeds the time, energy, and perceived skill that you have to accomplish it all. You may feel as if you are withering under the pressure. You're not getting enough sleep; you're not eating well; your mood is sour; and your relationship is taking a backseat. Fun and soulful connection are nowhere on the horizon.

In certain situations you might attempt to push yourself past your endurance level. While this strategy can sometimes work in the short run, overstriving is likely to deplete you or generate burnout over time. Loss of effectiveness and efficiency also tend to occur when you exceed your energy threshold—it is the law of diminishing returns.

How can you look your challenges in the eye and feel peace and calm amid the demands and commotion of daily life? Learning to attune to your inner guidance—putting Spirit, or whatever you call it, at the center—provides clarity about your priorities and your use of energy in any situation. The ability to find balance stems from dedication to living true to yourself and to drawing on your storehouse of self-love. Only from this position of authentic expression can you truly contribute to your marriage in a soulful way.

You, Me, and Us

Learning to grow in autonomy, character strength, and self-care can lead to more respect and cooperation with your spouse. In fact, couples who maintain a strong sense of you, me, and us have a better likelihood of sustaining a viable, enduring marriage. As you each stand true to who you are, you can be a genuine well-wisher for your partner and can increase your synergy as a couple.

Imagine two circles: One is you; one is your mate. How would you position the circles to show the overlap of you + me = us? Maintaining your separate identity *and* uniting with your partner may seem like a paradox. As a healthy couple, you can gradually learn to balance your individuality (separate as two) and your marriage's soulful oneness (one). You can call this the dance of the one and the two!

Here are a few examples of healthy personal activity and corresponding soulful couple behavior:

Personal	Couple
expressing/asserting needs or desires	mutual accommodation or compromise
working effectively on a task or project	synergy through collaboration
engaging in an interest or a hobby	pursuing an activity that both enjoy or value
resourceful problem solving	making an empowering joint decision
caring for a child or pet	cooperative parenting

Space Between: Ron and Mary

The composer Claude Debussy said, "Music is the space between the notes." We have learned that "space between" is an integral part of our harmonious marriage.

Our Saturday morning is under way. Mary walks the dogs while Ron checks email. Later, after Mary's yoga and belly-dance classes, she meets a friend for some girl time. Meanwhile, Ron takes the dogs on walk number two (no pun intended), then joins his buddies for tennis-team practice. Afterward, Ron mows three lawns as part of his small landscape business.

During the evening, we sit on our deck to share our day, as Mary sips a glass of wine and Ron enjoys his bourbon on the rocks.

Mary: Early in our marriage, I thought Ron had to be "everything" to me. Fortunately, I learned the importance of caring for myself. Ron supports my decisions to take yoga, Pilates, and belly-dancing, to spend time with my friends, and even to travel on my own. It's not that I *need* his permission; it's that I *love* his support.

Ron: I enjoy the time Mary and I spend together after we have been apart. When I get home from a tennis match, a woodturning club meeting, or lunch with a friend, I have lots of new stuff to share. Last year, Mary went to Mexico to do yoga with friends. When she returned, we engaged in hours of conversation about how we had spent our time apart, what we learned, and planning for the future.

By supporting each other to pursue separate interests and allowing for the space between, each of us has had the opportunity to grow as individuals and as a couple during our forty-four-year marriage.

Honoring your true self takes many forms, including making space for important alone time, apart from your spouse. Taking time to rest, meditate, and pray alone, or to play and laugh with friends, is enriching. When you spend time with your own friends, have separate hobbies, and give each other some breathing room, you are each more energized when you get back together. You are then much more interesting to your partner than when you're merely talking about your job or news reports and listing things to do. Having time apart allows you each the space to develop personally and to appreciate one another. As you take good care of yourself, you are more likely to develop into an exciting, engaging lover.

Shift in Consciousness

Conventional Model: Taking Care of Yourself Is Selfish

You should take care of others and make sure that they are happy, even if you sacrifice your health and happiness in the process. Looking outside yourself to help others is more noble than looking inside yourself for what you need.

Soulful Model: Self-Care Benefits Others

Fill yourself first and give from the overflow. Focusing on personal growth and developing your capacity to love and be loved makes you more available to others, and less likely to get emotionally, physically, or spiritually depleted. Taking care of yourself helps seal your leaks and gives you more energy to share with others.

Shoring up your self-love can also include activities that you share with your partner. Hugging, making love, exploring new places, sharing faith-based activities, and expressing gratitude for what you have in life together are wonderful ways to fill your love vessel. What are some of your favorite ways to honor yourself, both by yourself and with your beloved?

Spirit in the Center: Jim and Ruth

One of the most magical secrets of our soulful marriage is that we have shared the same religious and spiritual journey since birth. Growing up in Jewish homes, we each have a strong appreciation of our roots, love Jewish prayers and rituals, and enjoy celebrating the Sabbath and the many Jewish holidays with our family. Even in grade school, we felt mystically connected to God. Brimming with curiosity, we each raised numerous questions during the humble beginnings of our search for the truth.

While remaining practitioners of the Jewish faith throughout our lives, we have relished the joy and depth of discovering truths from many traditions and faiths. We are fortunate to have had wonderful teachers, coaches, mentors, and guides in holistic health, wellness, healing, humanistic and transpersonal psychology, yoga, and Sufi studies. We are amazed how compatible we have been in our ongoing joint spiritual ventures since the 1970s, and feel extremely blessed to walk side by side on the spiritual journey as we celebrate our personal lessons along the way.

Upon arising and before bedtime, we carve out time for spiritual practice and prayer; sometimes we recite brief prayers together at other times of the day. We have the ongoing pleasure of sharing classes, intensives, retreats, service projects, and special gatherings with our current Jewish and Sufi communities. The two of us serve together as kinship directors of the Front Range Sufi Order International and as Jewish meditation leaders (rotating with two others) at a synagogue in Denver. We have just completed a two-year intensive healing conductors program.

Our spiritual focus provides an anchor that guides all our life choices. The confluence of our spiritual paths also serves as a vehicle for peacemaking, for interfaith respect, and for championing unity through diversity—a central life purpose for both of us. Furthermore, we are very pleased to have raised spiritually attuned, openhearted children and we consciously guide our grandchildren to appreciate the bountiful gifts of life.

An important element in achieving balance in your life is recognizing when stress is throwing things out of balance, and then taking action to restore it. Sometimes the causes of stress are easy to identify and the corrections are relatively simple—refocusing on healthy choices, reactivating good communication, and rededicating yourself to spiritual practices that nurture your soul. Other times it may require the help of counseling or coaching—either alone or together—to pinpoint the causes of stress and the solutions to alleviate it.

Shift in Consciousness

Conventional Model: Hard Work Is Valued

Work hard, put in long hours, be highly productive, earn a lot of money—these are the keys to success. Wait for the weekends, vacations, and retirement to really relax. Life is full of struggles and hardships. Prepare for the worst and hope for the best.

Soulful Model: Value Your Work

Value and enjoy your work. Express your gifts and talents and relate well to others. Success involves the balance of being, doing, and having. Taking time each day to stop, rest, and reflect builds personal and marital resilience.

Our Balanced Relationship: Dante and Claudia

Our marriage is a blessing. The first few months seemed perfect; we were so excited to finally spend our life together. Then we realized how everything was changing in our lives. We were way out of balance, as our activities and priorities had drastically changed from when we were single. We were not eating healthily or sleeping and exercising enough. As a result, we were continually tired, grumpy, and unmotivated—a far cry from perfect. We started looking for that balance and discovered that simple activities and changes were the key to enjoying each other's company, as well as having personal time.

> We want to share what works for us:
>
> We follow a nutrition plan and cook healthy food together. Doing this is not only beneficial to our bodies but also to our relationship, since we discuss our day and our future plans while preparing meals.
>
> We exercise together at least four days a week, which helps us feel more energetic, happier, and more motivated, focused, and productive. We encourage and challenge each other when we're working out.
>
> We practice gratitude and visualization prayers during mornings and nights together. Doing so has helped us attract greater feelings of abundance and meaning into our lives.
>
> We frequently discuss our personal, professional, and financial goals, and are working on our family vision. This allows us to be on the same page and stay focused on where we are heading as a family.

Our marriage now feels truly fulfilling to each of us.

Sanctifying Your Choices

Dante and Claudia are models of the power of determination and collaboration to restore balance. You value yourself and your beloved. When you each consciously determine the best use of your resources, your course of action in any given situation becomes clear. Clarity also results from having your virtues or principles front and center in making everyday and longer-range decisions. Taking time to develop agreements and guidelines can help you each feel affirmed and secure. Knowing that you are validating your common ground and accommodating your differences can build marital strength and resilience.

Some couples develop a code of ethics, a mission statement, or a list of pillars or guiding principles. Come up with your own way of expressing what is essential to you. Base your solutions on sanctifying your choices within your relationship. For example, you may take a strong stand for peace, so when you are faced with a conflict between the two of you, you seek to resolve underlying differences, and look for constructive alternatives that will solve the problem and build the relationship. If you place a premium on education, you might devote time to volunteering at your children's school or, if you don't have children, mentoring at a school in your community.

Helpful questions to guide you in developing your shared code of ethics include "What best serves me and us in this matter?" and "Does this choice represent a good use of my/our time, energy, or money?"

Balanced Home, Balanced Life

Another set of choices and an opportunity for life balance involves the division of labor in your home. Home can be a sanctuary or a stressful place. If it is chaotic, it can drain your energy, affect your health, and jeopardize your overall well-being. Knowing that you each have your own way of handling things, how can you manage your household to produce a sense of peace and balance at home?

What if you allocate household chores so you bring out your best selves? Who is good at managing money? time? space? energy? Build a team approach to play to your strengths and interests. One of you may find inspiration in home decor while the other enjoys beautifying the yard. You may want to alternate weeks doing the cooking, cleaning, shopping, laundry, and entertaining. Determine what best suits your time and interests. Who has the skills and desires better geared to handling finances? managing the vehicles? doing household repairs? Be realistic, as well as thinking outside the box, in deciding who does what.

Try to vary the tasks, so that one person pays bills the first fifteen days of the month and the other pays the bills at the end of the month, for example. Change it around when you get bored or have more energy for new projects.

Juggling and Balancing: Connie and Ross

My husband and I are building two successful, home-based businesses during, arguably, the most challenging economy of our lifetime. Maintaining sanity while juggling marriage and children, and running a household and two businesses can be quite difficult at times. But we have found that the rewards are well worth the effort. We view our thriving businesses as extensions of our successful marriage.

When a couple works together, particularly in a home-based business, the line between home life and work life can blur. Some people are very adept at keeping the two separate. My husband and I tend to be a little less linear in our thinking, so mixing it all together seems to work best for us. Regardless of what may be going on in our work lives, we still have a household to run and children to raise. As we are never off the clock, we are free to talk business whenever and wherever the mood strikes. We have some of our best business meetings over glasses of wine in the hot tub or over morning coffee in the backyard.

Also, we find that it is vitally important to periodically take a little *me* time to be alone with ourselves. This could be as simple as taking a walk, going out for coffee, getting a massage, or reading a book on a park bench.

Communication is the area that we work on the most. Often in trying to convince the other of a particular point, we eventually realize that we actually have the same opinion; we just express it in very different ways. We may disagree on the route to take but generally we agree on the destination. Frankly, we tend to both want to be in charge, so yielding control is never easy. Maximizing personal talents allows each of us to be the "alpha dog" in those aspects of business in which we excel. When we remove ego from the equation, the result is greater harmony, cooperation, and efficiency. Maintaining a sense of humor and perspective is crucial— it is only business, after all!

At the end of the day, we do what we do because we believe in the entrepreneurial spirit. We want to do good in the world and to create something lasting for our children. It is not always easy, but it is always worth it. There is no one we would rather build businesses with than each other.

Organizing the responsibilities of the home goes far toward helping to achieve balance. When home is a place where you can express your true self and celebrate your partner's genuine gifts, it can be experienced as a holy sanctuary and a fountain of love.

Integrating Masculine and Feminine Traits

Traditional views regarding male and female behaviors and roles can be restrictive. Men do the "masculine" intellectual tasks—handling finances and decision making—and women do the "feminine" emotional tasks, such as cooking, homemaking, and child-rearing. In the traditional view we mentioned in chapter 4, men are thought of as the head and women the body, so by putting the two halves together you get one whole person. Marriages have been based on this premise for centuries, mostly because households tend to survive with an efficient chain of command. Watch old movies and television shows to see the stereotypes exemplified.

> Happiness in not a matter of intensity, but of balance and order and rhythm and harmony.
>
> —Thomas Merton,
> *No Man Is an Island*

But this outdated model may handicap and demoralize the human spirit. We are each made whole by a balance of masculine and feminine qualities. In applying principles of soulful living, you are free to express all aspects of yourself. As you develop and display your masculine and feminine traits, you become a balanced, well-integrated person with breadth and depth. Supporting your inner wholeness and your partner's creates a strong, respectful, and soulful marriage: 1 + 1 = many possibilities.

Below is an extensive array of prototypical masculine and feminine qualities. Notice which features are most prominent in you and which ones are less characteristic of you.

Masculine Energy	Feminine Energy
Active	Receptive
Autonomous	Relational
Wielding power over others	Sharing power
Aggressive	Assertive
Focused	Flowing
Outer-directed	Inner-directed
Intellectual	Emotional
Analytical	Intuitive
Competitive	Collaborative
Penetrating	Nurturing
Goal-oriented	Open-ended; process-oriented
Convergent	Divergent
Hierarchical	Consensual
Yang	Yin

Quickly review the list of various gender characteristics above. Instead of trying to decide whether you are either this or that, experiment with using the inclusive word *and*. Accept yourself as having masculine *and* feminine traits. This way, energy is not wasted on internal conflict. Have you noticed that when you expand your range of behaviors, more positive possibilities are available to you?

Evolving into a whole person allows you to more smoothly navigate through the following dimensions:

Inner *and* outer focus

Being alone *and* together

Experiencing yourself as introverted *and* extroverted

Being adept at planning *and* spontaneity

Thinking *and* feeling

Being responsible *and* frivolous

Acting as a capable adult *and* a creative child

Being active *and* receptive

Using your cup *and* sword

Extreme behavior patterns and emotional reactions detract from balanced, healthy functioning. Alternating from one extreme to the other can be especially destabilizing for you and your relationship. Learn to do everything in moderation, including practicing moderation itself. In a given situation, be like Goldilocks, who discerned what was too much of something or too little of it; she sensed what was just right.

Small Self, Greater Self

Having a vital spiritual life is also important to achieving balance in your relationship. Strong spiritual connections can fortify your inner lives against wayward behavior and destructive self-talk. Often this kind of negative inner and outer behavior stems from what is called your small self. Getting caught up in the cultural mind-set that there is not enough— time, money, space, energy, love—is one example of the influence of your small self. This constricted way of thinking may spark feelings of anxiety, fear, inadequacy, and a sense of separation and aloneness. If either you or your partner—or, worse, both of you—is being overly influenced by your small self, the soulful nature of your union is bound to suffer.

Your aim as an individual and a couple is to quiet the small self so you can reconnect with the Greater Self, the source of abundance, gratitude, humility, respect, and love. Ask your partner to support you in your efforts to minimize self-talk and remarks about fear-based limitations. Request that your beloved collaborate with you in creating more harmony in your home by focusing on the spiritual dimensions of your relationship. Forgiving yourself and your partner for past ways of being imbalanced can free up enormous energy and bring more harmony to your relationship. Taking time to rest, observing the Sabbath or other refreshing days, being in silence, and engaging in spiritual practices can promote the integration of the small self with the Greater Self. Even a few hours or a few days can rebalance your spiritual rhythms.

Soulful Lives Need Social Lives

In the process of integrating the various dimensions of yourself, you are learning to be healthy and autonomous *and* in a vital relationship with your partner. As your trust in each other grows stronger, you deepen your relationship. With such soulful connection, your life purpose and reasons for being together may become increasingly clear. You have each other to support each other's central life purpose(s).

Your social relationships also serve as a vital form of support for you and your committed relationship. Your friends and close associates affirm you, individually and as a couple. They can serve as a reflective mirror of your inner and shared beliefs.

As you and your relationship grow and change, so too may your social circle. You might want to be with more people who are in balance and whose lives reflect your quest for soulful living. It is important to find social connections that enhance your new sense of awareness and commitment to authentic living. You can do this by taking classes, joining personal development groups, and seeking out stimulating and spiritually nourishing activities. Enjoy couple time through a variety of organized activities offered at churches, synagogues, temples, mosques, yoga studios, or spiritual centers, or through nature groups. Doing so may help you both feel connected with a community with which you have a sense of belonging, holiness, and service, and through which you can make a difference.

Laughter: The Great Leveler

A balanced life involves injecting levity into the busyness and routine of your mundane life. Various forms of fun, playfulness, and humor allow you to lighten up and regain perspective. Suppose you arrive home from work feeling tired, depleted, and cranky. Consider how you could shift your mood by acting silly, singing, playing a quick game, watching a sitcom, or reading an inspirational story—alone or with your partner. Having pet names for your partner can help shift the mood, too. With agreement not to hurt your dear one, you might say something like this if she comes home from work in a grumpy mood: "Uh-oh, here comes Cousin It. Better stay away until Joanie returns." Then she is free to go rest or pull weeds or have a cup of tea to re-center and come to inner balance.

Be sure to set time and space boundaries so that you have free time to enjoy yourself, your partner, and your family and social network, and fulfill your professional responsibilities. You might want to coach your partner to give you at least twenty minutes of downtime to transition from work to home and to be understanding when work needs to temporarily take precedence over your relationship. Schedule make-up time to do something special after you return from your work demands. Realize that you are clearly out of balance if you are consistently making work your top priority. As a spiritual teacher once said, "If you make things [such as your work] more important than yourself [people], you create insanity."

Togetherness can be delicious and precious and it must be balanced with strong inner lives, healthy lifestyle choices, a peaceful home environment, vital spiritual connections, and a refreshing dose of humor to be truly soulful.

TAKING ACTION

Personal Practice: Centered versus Off Balance

Arrange a quiet moment to reflect. Turn off all distractions and be alone for twenty minutes or so. Focus on your breathing, without trying to change it. As your mind quiets and your body relaxes, your breath comes into its own natural rhythm. Once you feel the sense of peace inside, label this *home, my quiet place,* or whatever name works for you. Use a journal or word document to describe this state of being. For example: *calm, confident, serene, luscious, clear, loving, at peace, sexy, my soul, my true self.*

Now imagine what you are like when you are stressed, overwhelmed, anxious, or upset. Label this state of being *away from home, my squirrely place,* or *crazyland.* Let yourself feel and recognize this condition of being far from your true self. Name the traits you possess at your time of stress. For example: *anxious, irritable, withdrawn, aggressive, inconsolable, stressed, tired, unmotivated.*

Experience the contrast of the *home* space and the *away* space. List ways to build bridges to return *home.* For example, take a walk, meditate, cry, call a friend, exercise, pray, write, dance, or cook.

Personal Practice: Bring Balance to Your Week

I, Jim, recently realized the impact of my mother's oft-repeated adage, "Man cannot live by bread alone" on my adult choices. Shortly after graduating from college, I concluded that many working adults were functioning like hamsters on a wheel. Upon entering my career at age twenty-three, I resolved to avoid ruts, such as watching television on a nightly basis. Instead, I incorporated various forms of reading, exercise, and creativity into my life. I also allotted time for socializing, prayer, and spontaneity—occasionally doing things on a lark or being silly. In my thirties, I added parenting, mysticism, and community service as vital endeavors. Since I am continually nourished by this range of pursuits, I cannot imagine living less than a multifaceted existence.

How about you? Describe your range of activities and what helps you feel most balanced. What are you willing to include this week?

Personal Practice: Life Infused by Spirit

Here is a way to create a visual representation of a balanced life. You might want to get out your crayons or markers for this one.

Draw a circle on a page, label the center *Spirit,* then extend four to eight rays out from the center, one to represent each of the various areas of your life. Primary examples of rays that you could consider are:

Physical: body care, home care, work, finances

Emotional: feelings, social skills, relationships, past hurts, desires, dreams

Mental: attitudes, beliefs, intellect, learning abilities, memory, intuition

Community and Social: friends and acquaintances, support, service, faith community

Recreation or Fun: hobbies, interests, playful activities, vacations

Activism: politics, environmental concerns, education

Creativity: art, music, dance, writing

Take a few moments to label the rays with words, colors, or symbols.

Now visualize the hollow center of the circle as your life energy, similar to the bright power of the sun. This is the solar power of your life.

Take a deep breath and visualize your in-breath illuminating the center of the circle and your outbreath sending energy out through the different rays.

Contemplate:

- Which areas of my life receive more energy?
- What am I willing to do to better focus on some other areas?
- Where or how is my energy leaking?
- What is in balance in my life?
- What is out of balance?

Share your diagram and your intentions with your partner as ways of expressing how you'd like to achieve better balance in your life. Being aware, motivated, and assertive empowers you to be true to yourself. Ask your honey to support you with loving accountability.

Personal Practice: Assessing Congruence

This exercise reflects your values and gives you a sense of how congruent your actual behavior is with your ideals. In your journal, draw horizontal lines for each category and label them at each end as shown below. On the line, indicate where you currently are with an X and where you want to be with a star.

Time

I need my day to be structured in order to be productive.	————————	I enjoy letting my day unfold to allow for spontaneity.
I carefully allocate time among my various activities.	————————	I allow whatever amount of time is required for each activity.

Space

I need to be alone most of the time.	————————	I prefer being with other people.
I enjoy wide-open spaces, like being in nature or large rooms.	————————	I like small, cozy spaces.

Energy

| I tend to use my energy quickly, then feel fatigued. | ———————————— | I pace myself and can stay fresh for a long time. |
| I often draw energy from others to sustain myself. | ———————————— | I allow life energy to flow freely through me. |

Money

| I am frugal and carefully budget my money. | ———————————— | I make my spending decisions in the moment. |
| I regularly save my money. | ———————————— | I tend to be a spendthrift. |

Soulful Connection: Comparing Notes

Compare your responses to the items with those of your partner. Does the location of your X's and stars surprise you? What are you learning about yourself and your dear one? Let the gap between your actual and ideal choices serve as substantive grist for a discussion. Perhaps your gap triggers some insights into your mate. For example, she might be critical of you or exert extra effort to compensate for your deficit in a certain area. Share your thoughts and feelings honestly.

Select one or two of the items that are calling out for your attention. Make a plan to close the gap between your actual and ideal way of dealing with your precious resources. Ask your partner to support you in specific ways. Help each other find balance in managing and sanctifying your choices.

Soulful Connection: Plan Your Work and Work Your Plan

Make a list of all your household tasks. Select your preferred ones and discuss your list with your mate. Here is a partial list; add you own items:

> Food: shopping, preparing, setting and clearing the table, cleaning up after meals, hosting parties, cleaning the refrigerator and the pantry

Money: earning, buying, saving, investing, bill paying, making donations

Cleaning: straightening, de-cluttering, dusting, vacuuming, washing laundry and clothing care

Child care (more in chapter 7 on parenting)

Pet care: feeding, walking, grooming, picking up excrement, taking pets to the veterinarian

Home maintenance: repairs, plumbing, painting, remodeling

Vehicles: buying gasoline, making repairs, doing scheduled maintenance, washing

Decorating and aesthetics

Outdoor care: lawn, trees and shrubbery, raking, snow-shoveling, gutter-cleaning

Celebrations and rituals: birthdays, anniversaries, holidays, ceremonies, gift-giving

Decide on the activities or areas for which you and your partner are taking responsibility. Perhaps you need to put these agreements in writing. Post the note or chart on the refrigerator or in another conspicuous place.

Hold each other accountable in kind yet firm ways. Arrange a trial period to test whether this is a good plan for your home. Start with two or three weeks. Keep talking about it as you go along without nagging, blaming, or criticizing. Remember to turn complaints into requests. Check in at the end of the trial period to revise or reinforce your ways of maintaining the household.

Household routines can become considerably disrupted during difficult periods or unforeseen events. You may need to make accommodations for each other in times of distress or crisis. Handling difficulties with skill and grace is essential. Either you or a family member may become injured, sick, be in the throes of financial or career upheaval, or grieving the loss of a loved one. How can the household run smoothly with these changes? Discuss your specific concerns and reassure each other that you can find workable solutions. Life can be a challenging—even cruel—teacher sometimes. How can you make the best of a difficult situation? Stay centered, review options, and seek help and support if additional guidance is required.

Soulful Connection: Your Masculine and Feminine Traits

Discuss the notion of masculine and feminine traits as shown in the chart on page 112. Add your own characteristics. Have fun with this topic during an evening discussion at dinner or on a walk-and-talk date. Consider the following points:

> What traits do you each want to activate to become more balanced and whole?

> How can you support each other in expressing and honoring every aspect of yourself?

> What qualities would you like to express more in your sensual and sexual love life? For example, are you, the man, willing to be a receptive partner in sex? Are you, the woman, willing to be active or dominant in lovemaking?

> How do you want to share the household duties in ways that best fit with your masculine and feminine qualities?

> How do you want to raise your children (or to support other children) with regard to masculine and feminine principles?

Personal Practice: Five-Element Breathing Meditation

Take ten to fifteen minutes to center yourself, meditate, and balance your four dimensions: physical, emotional, mental, and spiritual energies. This could become your morning and evening meditation practice.

Sit upright, with even weight on your tailbone and sitting bones. Align the top of your head with your tailbone. Relax your eyes, jaw, and neck. Stack your ears over your shoulders, and your shoulders over your hips. Inhale from your lower belly to the top of your chest; exhale down to your belly (like filling and emptying a glass). Allow the in-breath and the out-breath to stroke your heart gently, as if with a feather. Inhale to awaken your conscious mind; exhale to further relax down into your body.

Do five inhalation-exhalation cycles for each of the following elements, which correspond to the four dimensions stated above.

Earth

Inhaling through the nose, draw the breath up from the earth, through your tailbone to the top of your head, as if through a hollow column. Let your bones, muscles, organs, tissues, nerves, and brain be nourished. Exhale through your nose, down through the spinal column, releasing through the tailbone area, back into the earth.

Water

As you inhale through your nose, picture water entering through the top of your head. Exhale out the mouth, rinsing and purifying your body's liquids (blood, lymph, other fluids), sensing the water flowing out of your hands and feet.

Fire

As you visualize glowing coals being stoked in the solar plexus, strongly inhale through the mouth. Exhale through the nose, allowing the breath to rise to the chest and exit the heart as warm, loving energy.

Air

Imagine the pores of the skin open, allowing the inhale through the mouth to create more space inside. Exhale through the mouth, extending your energy in all directions.

Ether

The organic compound ether integrates the energies of the other four elements. Very softly inhaling and exhaling through the nose, imagine gently circulating a refined mist of healing air through your body.

Slowly come back to the present moment. Gently stretch your body and awaken from your meditation. Use your journal to record any messages or insights that you want to track.

Soulful Connection: Designing Your Sabbath

Make an agreement with your beloved to take time together away from work, house projects, errands, media, phones, and other people's agendas in order to replenish and spiritually nourish yourselves. Allow this Sabbath—no matter what day or how often you arrange it—to be filled with rest, study, time in nature, making love, prayer, meditation, light exercise, walks. Prepare yourself by doing the following:

Putting the date on your calendar when you will observe your special Sabbath together.

Creating a statement of intention for how you want to spend the day together.

Avoiding mundane activities that are likely to distract you or to demand your attention.

Telling family or friends you will not be available (e.g., to answer your phone or respond to emails).

Upon completing your Sabbath together, evaluate what you liked and did not enjoy about the experience. Decide whether you want to continue with a weekly, monthly, or quarterly Sabbath observance. What aspects of your retreat time were especially satisfying? You both could benefit from periodically arranging an extended retreat, such as a marriage enrichment retreat or sustained time to be in nature, reflect, talk, and read.

Sustaining Your Soulful Relationship While Parenting

Cultivating Couple Care

Everyone needs a house to live in, but a supportive
family is what builds a home.

—Anthony Liccione, *Back Words and Forward*

Setting up house with your best friend is a dream come true. Out of
your love for each other, you may decide to parent children to share in
and enrich your life. The early days of having a baby in your world are
filled with overwhelming joy, gratitude, and awe at the miracle of life. As
your children grow, your love and appreciation of them and each other
often grow deeper.

Of course, child-rearing is also fraught with challenges and demands.
Raising children requires a lot of attention and energy, which often
infringes on your couple time. In the face of running a household, working, and parenting, the imperative to stay aware of your own and your

partner's needs and feelings may bring on stress. Fatigue can be overwhelming, but with good self-care, couple care, and a grateful heart you can thrive as parents and as soulful partners.

This chapter focuses on ways to support each other to maintain a soulful relationship amid effective parenting. While guidelines and methods for soulful parenting and healthy child development are beyond the scope of this book (but stay tuned!), we'll show you how having a shared vision and working collaboratively to raise spiritually aware children is a secret to sustaining a soulful marriage.

Staying Soulful Involves Planning

Introducing a new member into your family creates emotions, chaos, and difficulties that may take you by surprise. Kids push your buttons. You push theirs. Your marriage may fracture apart or grow stronger once children arrive. While your children may be testing you, the overall challenges of parenting could be testing your relationship. You can choose to use it all to grow and unfold. Children certainly give parents a wonderful opportunity to practice unconditional love. Expanding your capacity to love then flows into your intimate relationship with your beloved.

Ideally, you talk with your beloved about approaches to child-rearing and your philosophies and visions of being a close couple with child(ren) before starting your family. Read books, talk with other parents, take classes, and listen to audiobooks or podcasts so you feel more prepared for the impact children will have on your relationship. As your children grow and develop, keep talking with your partner about your reactions to the changes in yourself and in your relationship, as well as discussing your evolving views and styles of parenting.

Shift in Consciousness

Conventional Model: Be Consistent at All Times

This has been the conventional wisdom for the past generations: Consistent child-rearing practices are essential for effective parenting. Parents should present a united front and not show any disagreements. As a couple, you know what to do in all situations and your children should obey you at all times. Parents have the final word, with no room for negotiation.

Soulful Model: Be Present, Skillful, and Flexible

Effective parenting requires fluidly adapting to personality differences, temperaments, moods, and circumstances. Your children are learning by watching you. As a soulful couple, you are intent on learning new relationship and communication skills that, in turn, affect your children. They pick up on your expanding repertoire of ways to constructively manage emotions and disagreements.

Many twentieth-century authorities on parenting preached the importance of consistent standards, rules, modeling, and behavior. Indeed, children can become confused and unsettled by vacillation and mixed messages, so it is helpful for parents to get on the same page regarding core values, behavior codes, and disciplinary measures.

However, in the twenty-first-century soulful approach to parenting it is highly unrealistic to believe that you should or could maintain unwavering uniformity in child-rearing, any more than you could remain impeccable in any other area of life. Parenting styles can certainly differ, which is natural and okay. As a couple you may disagree, then find common ground that enables you to forge a solution beyond either one of your points of view. Operating from a rigid framework instills anxiety, guilt, and shame. Flexibility, including experimenting with new approaches, enhances parenting as a soulful couple. When you are present, discerning, and skillful in any given situation, you serve your family better.

Some couples find it helpful to set aside time to create parenting agreements. These may include who does what and when, as well as shared philosophies and expectations. Being clear on your personal beliefs, convictions, and models of raising children can give added force to these agreements. Decide together what is acceptable and what is not. For example, one partner might say, "We must agree in front of the kids; we cannot let them see us fight" while the other contends that "We can talk over what is going on and disagree in front of our children. Our focus is to find the best way to handle a situation." Speaking and listening during a calm time, before any incidents that need addressing, can help you understand your partner's parenting style and come up with some general agreements that can be revised as life changes. You may notice that prior to having children, your approach to parenting mirrored your parents' style. But now, with a little experience, you may not agree with that approach. Allow your awareness to expand and grow. Plan to revisit your parenting agreements on a regular basis to check in with your partner and make adjustments that reflect your experience and growth.

Problem-Solve as Partners

Marriage research shows that the highest predictor of relationship longevity is the ability to constructively resolve conflicts and set clear boundaries. As an added benefit, your children witness you effectively resolving everyday conflicts together and, by witnessing this, gain a sense of trust and security. Setting firm and reasonable limits establishes order and structure. Creating a culture of fairness and respect allays the fight-flight-freeze reactions and paves the way for effective guidance and discipline.

Constructive problem solving as a couple can enhance self-esteem and build stability in your relationship and in your home. Your spouse and children are more inclined to forgive your idiosyncrasies and imperfections when you communicate clearly, offer fair solutions, and build self-confidence. Remember, your kids are observing you and modeling your marital and parenting interactions. Through your positive efforts, each of you can feel that you're contributing to the greater welfare of your family and community.

Developing Balance with Your Partner and Your Family

As parents, it is natural to want to devote much of your time to caring for and providing for your children. However, complete immersion in your children can backfire if you do not devote ample time to nurturing yourself and your marriage. Consider how many couples you know who regularly exhaust themselves by watching, leading, or coaching a number of their children's extracurricular activities each week, in addition to all the requisite driving time.

Shift in Consciousness

Conventional Model: Child-Centered Family

Devote the bulk of your resources—time, attention, energy, and money—to providing for your children's needs and desires. Give all you can to your children so they do not feel deprived or unloved. Take care of them by sacrificing what you need.

Soulful Model: Couple-Centered Family

Your family functions best when you and your spouse treat your relationship as primary, keeping your bond strong. As an outgrowth of your intimate connection, you can sufficiently attend to your children's needs and desires. Your children are nurtured by the loving foundation that you provide.

Child-centered couples often burn out from excessive devotion to the children. They do not allocate adequate resources to replenishing themselves. Couple care, a term for self-care of your partnership, is vital in parenting. This is especially true if you have a large family and/or special-needs children, such as those with learning difficulties or physical or emotional disabilities.

A few examples of quick, yet effective couple care actions you can do together include taking a ten-minute power nap, doing breathing exercises together, tenderly holding each other, and jointly reading and discussing a section of a parenting book. Taking time to celebrate the many joys of parenting together is also easy and important. Acknowledge milestones, such as the awe you feel at some of your child's first experiences, major achievements, and special occasions. You can even share your appreciation of witnessing your child show kindness to others or her gratitude for the natural world.

Over the long term, you and your partner prosper by developing your own individual and shared interests and hobbies. This includes taking some vacations, if only the occasional weekend, apart from your children.

Participation in a mutually trusting community can enhance the quality of your life. Receiving emotional and practical support from others is essential to maintaining your well-being and healthy balance as a couple and to promoting your family's overall well-being. Being part of a community allows you to share parenting duties with other adults and thus have more couple time. Sleepovers and vacations with friends and family can free up time and space for you to be alone as a couple. Children flourish when they are nurtured and encouraged by an extended network of grandparents, other relatives, caregivers, family friends, and community members. Hillary Clinton popularized the African proverb, "It takes a village to raise a child."

Frequently carving out time to communicate with your mate about your own needs, wants, plans, priorities, and goals, as well as those of your family, is an integral part of family well-being. When you dedicate downtime and quality sustained time to yourself and your beloved, you model balance and mutual support for your family. Everyone has the potential to thrive.

Planting Seeds for Our Children: Tom and Carrie

When we consider the stages our marriage goes through over a lifetime, the years of being busy raising children are some of our most rewarding but also some of the most demanding. We find ourselves stretched thin with work and family obligations, and often have little time to connect with each other. At the same time, some of our sweetest moments are those spent with everyone in the family together, playing a sport or a game, taking a trip, or simply sharing a meal. We try to remain close, or even grow closer, during this period.

When our boys were young we often had very little free time. When they were finally in bed, it was tempting to do our own individual tasks, rather than spending time with each other. Inevitably, we ended up feeling more distant and disconnected. We decided that we would make time for each other first. Most of the other stuff truly could wait. Often our dates were just sitting on the couch talking to each other. We nurtured our friendship through those simple times.

Ultimately we teach our kids more through our actions than through our words. The environment in our home is created in simple ways. We hug and kiss each other when we get home from work, and neither of us enters or leaves our home unnoticed. We let our kids see us disagree at times, and we work to respectfully resolve our differences. They see us taking time to listen to each other. All these small things plant the seeds for our kids to grow up and have their own healthy, thriving marriage.

Instilling Important Messages

Make sure that you and your spouse collaborate to instill messages that foster healthy self-esteem and self-confidence. Verbally and nonverbally, consciously and unconsciously, you continually transmit a host of messages to your spouse and your children. They are adept at perceiving even covert messages from you, some of which may not serve them well. Guard self-worth so that each of you matures with a strong sense of your inherent value, brimming with confidence and competence. Equalize and balance the power as a soulful couple to promote stability and peace in the home. Key examples of positive messages to impart to your beloved and your children include:

- I deeply love and care for you.
- You are capable. I believe in you.
- I trust in you.
- Right now, you have my full attention.
- I know that you can handle this. Ask me if you want any support.
- I encourage you to be true to yourself.
- We disagree right now, so let's find a solution that solves the problem and builds our relationship.
- Even though we have different perspectives, we can learn from each other.
- Let me know how you are feeling and what you need.
- All your feelings are welcome and acceptable. Please learn healthy ways to express them.

Shift in Consciousness

Conventional Model: Keep Your Child Controlled

Old models of child-rearing warned parents to maintain control of their children. Misbehavior was seen as wrong, bad, and a poor reflection on the parents. They were told not to praise their children because too much positive attention would give their children inflated egos. The guidance was, "Just reprimand what is wrong and don't comment if your children are behaving properly." Use guilt and shame as tactics to manage your children's behavior.

Soulful Model: Offer Structure and Freedom

Children (and all of us) need strong egos to weather the storms of life and to value successes. Generously give them the tools they need to make their way in life. As your kids become more adept at facing challenges, they develop confidence and self-esteem. Misbehavior is considered a reflection of unmet needs and is indicative of skills that are yet to be learned. You can use the misbehavior as a teachable moment.

Reinforcing desired behavior and effort is more meaningful and credible than global praise, like "You are so great." Instead, try statements such as "I am so happy that you cleaned out the garage today. It looks so organized. Thank you. High five!" This applies to your adult love relationship as well.

As with your children, speaking respectfully and affectionately to your partner deepens your bond. Acknowledging each other doing something right is much more effective than picking on faults and shortcomings. Your relationship with your beloved—and your family unit as a whole—can be strengthened by sharing kind words and loving gestures. Activate a healthy home life by honoring the five love languages (from chapter 4) and valuing varied forms of connection with one another.

Your Child's Life Is Not Your Own

You may want to educate yourselves about the stages of child development so that you have realistic expectations and can assist your child in moving fluidly from one stage to another. As you learn more about physical, emotional, mental, moral, and spiritual development, you may gain insight into your own childhood and that of your spouse. You may notice that as your child reaches a certain age or milestone, your own pent-up emotions or unpleasant memories from that time are triggered. Ongoing discussions as a couple or with a counselor may help you resolve lingering issues from your own upbringing.

Be wary of trying to solve your children's problems or to live vicariously through them, in an effort to resolve your own issues from the past. Refer to the tools from the "Getting Personal" and "Breaking Loose" chapters to help you release old patterns. Seek counsel for difficulties that are mounting beyond what you can manage. Do you trust your partner enough to share with him these intimate details of your emotional inner life?

There are many resources—courses, books, podcasts, parent support groups, and seminars—to help you broaden your repertoire of child-rearing skills. Discuss with your partner what you are learning and how to put your insights into action with your children. Staying connected as an informed couple serves your child's development and your own healing.

Dealing with Challenging Circumstances

The journey of a soulful couple inevitably involves rough patches. During difficult marital times, be sure to safeguard your child's welfare. You may experience distress, such as losing a job, suffering from relationship conflicts, and struggling through health setbacks. Children can cope with discord if it is handled responsibly and with awareness. Putting your child in the middle of your adult conflicts is an unhealthy practice. Avoid speaking disrespectfully about the other parent in front of or to the children. Imprinting these negative messages can affect your children's well-being now and in the future—and deepen the wedge between you and your partner. Children become anxious about having to divide their loyalty and feel inadequate to resolve adult issues. It is also unfair to children to place them in the role of mediator or caretaker. Maintain the primary relationship with the adults as partners and parents. Your children need to live as kids, with your protective shield and safety net.

Your Children Also Face Hard Times

As adults grappling with so many responsibilities, you might sometimes (or often) forget that your children have plenty of their own issues and concerns. These can be stressful, painful—even terrifying—for your children and for you as parents. Discuss with your mate ways in which you can work together to deal most effectively and lovingly with challenges that are relevant to your family. Knowing that you are in it together as loving, supportive partners can help reduce the panic and helplessness commonly associated with such concerns. Here is a sample of issues that children and teens commonly confront:

- Health challenges, major illnesses, injuries, physical abnormalities, low immune function

- Body image concerns, eating disorders, allergies

- Anxiety or depression, obsessive-compulsive thoughts and behaviors

- Night terrors, sleep disturbances

- Learning disabilities; academic and behavioral problems at school

- Difficulties with peers, such as nonacceptance, taunting, bullying

- Parents separating or divorcing; death of a family member, friend, or pet; a friend moving away

- Sibling or parental abuse or neglect

- Addictive or risky behaviors

- School or community violence

When your child is dealing with a challenge or an adversity, she may require considerable attention and support from both of you. This can drain your energy and put a strain on your relationship. Make sure you get enough sleep, spend sufficient time with each other as a couple, and socialize with other supportive adults. Your child's challenge has the potential to serve as a spiritual teaching. The adversities may be met with compassion, kindness, honesty, and boundary setting. The darkest moments may open into the greatest light; unexpected breakthroughs may follow major breakdowns. Trust inner knowing and spiritual attunement to guide you. Being able to give words to your child's dark journey can allow her to move through it faster and with mindfulness. Strive to be a model of resourcefulness and resilience to help your child surmount these challenges.

As a couple, stay attuned to your beloved's emotions, needs, and special requests as you face these major stressors. Handling challenging, stressful events is a real test of your commitment to being your best selves (and accepting your lesser selves). How can you become more effective as mates and as parents during difficult times? Being attuned to what is going on, forgiving yourself and your beloved for overreactions or poor responses, making proactive decisions, and taking focused action can help ease the way. As an influential leadership trainer poignantly declared, "Adversity is the canvas upon which you paint your greatness."

Knowing when you need help and asking for it are signs of humility and graciousness. Letting others support you is a gift to all concerned. It is fine to reach out to others in your community for yourself, your child, or you and your partner as a couple. You are wise to draw on the resources of school personnel, counselors, health care providers, parent groups, social service agencies, and clergy.

Stepparenting and Blended Families

Not every marriage or relationship lasts a lifetime. Some marriages end when the partners outgrow each other, want different lifestyles, or grapple with circumstances that destroy the fiber of the relationship. Here are a few guidelines to help you maintain your own current love relationship, while dealing with the dissolution of your former marriage.

Stepfamilies, especially relatively new ones, often experience a plethora of trials, adjustments, and chaos. As the family reconstitutes itself, its emotional well-being centers around the strength of the adults' bond—the couple relationship needs to be the primary one in the family. As your bond with your new spouse grows stronger, the children's needs and concerns are likely to be better addressed; consequently, kids in the new, blended family tend to feel happier and more secure.

Of course, everyone benefits when tension and conflicts with your former spouse are dealt with peacefully and constructively. Keep your focus on proactive communication and on forging fair agreements that all parties honor. If your divorce was not amicable, you and your former spouse may need to communicate strictly by email and text message for a while, addressing nothing but matters concerning logistics and the children's welfare.

Be aware that your new spouse may resent what she perceives as your excessive attention to communicating with your former spouse. Be sensitive to one another's feelings and concerns, and make special time to connect with each other in playful, sexy, and nurturing ways. Try to avoid allowing the pain of your past relationship to seep into your current one. Have "ex-free" times when you do not discuss the past relationship or its effect on the present. Addressing issues with your former spouse as a constant diet can cause bitterness and resentment. Declare certain dates as time for fun, pleasure, relaxation, sacredness, or dream-building as a couple. Strengthen your current relationship by applying the secrets of a soulful marriage and learn from your past mistakes.

Grandparenting and the Empty Nest

What a grand delight and privilege it is to be a grandparent! You have the luxury of enjoying your grandchildren, especially during prolonged visits, without having to raise them or to provide for their daily needs. As a mature, stable, and wise elder, you can be a strong influence on and support to both your adult children and your grandchildren. You may notice your hearts swelling with joy and pride as you interact with your child's child. Having fun together brightens your day. It may seem like just a few years ago that you were teaching your child to ride a bike and now here you are running down the street together with your grandson as he learns to ride his bike. How fast time passes!

After a visit with your grandchild, you may feel closer to your beloved, as you recount the funny things the toddler did or the brilliant information your school-aged grandchild shared with you. Enjoying your empty nest can strengthen your soulful marriage immensely. Finding renewed energy for playing, laughing, creating, and exploring with your grandchildren can revitalize your intimacy with your partner.

As grandparents, your life together may seem brighter and more enjoyable. Sharing holidays, religious prayers, songs, and traditions can offer richness that binds you closer together. Transmitting your family legacies and rituals to your children's children may give you a sense of purpose and connection to your spiritual heritage. Tender moments of reflection may amplify your love and appreciation of each other.

The Joys of Grandparenting: Ellen and Marty

Watching with awe and cherishing firsts.

Playing boo boo (peek-a-boo) around the kitchen island, punctuated by belly laughs.

Little feet running jubilantly into open arms for big hugs and kisses.

Reading voraciously while snuggling on the sofa or tucked under the covers, taking time for questions and explanations.

Back rubs before bed and endearing words, such as "Grandma, why can't you move in?" and "It's hard to wait four days to see someone you love."

Transmitting our love of our culture through singing, dancing, contemporary spiritual services, and family traditions.

Building imagination through Legos, Lincoln Logs, wooden blocks, Trios, Magna-tiles, and more.

Annual outings to model train shows, the stock show, and the amusement park—hesitant at first, then higher, faster, and braver!

Train trips to the mountains, captivated by the scenery, intrigued by the tunnels, and bonded by the special time together, including playing miniature golf, playing board games, skipping rocks, and exploring the nooks and crannies of the motel.

Glorious fall days at the Pumpkin Patch, navigating the corn maze with kettle corn and funnel cake.

Touring a frontier farmhouse, churning butter, taking a hayride, and running carefree across sunlit fields.

Raking while "the leaves are dancing," interspersed with leaf fights and laughter.

Experiments like drying grapes to raisins on the windowsill.

Sharing our past and answering questions, such as "How did you and Grandpa meet?" followed by, "Why did you go out with someone you didn't know?"

Grandparents can give undivided attention, broad perspective, wisdom, and unconditional love, mixed with hugs, kisses, and tickles that create lifelong bonds.

Being elders in your empty nest can also bring various shared challenges to work through together. Caring for your health and finances and making important decisions about home, work, retirement, funeral plans, and leaving your legacy may be stressful, yet also draw you closer together. You are less inclined to grieve your children's departure from home and much more likely to enjoy this later stage of life if you and your mate have spent a lot of quality time together as you raised your children.

Magic in Everyday Miracles

Creating and sustaining a loving, sacred relationship may be one of your greatest accomplishments in this life. When life at home is satisfying and rich, the energy flows into all areas of your existence. Being parents together can unite you in ways that are hard to describe. Silent appreciation and heartfelt gratitude can deepen quiet moments together.

Children are small vehicles for their big souls. They can touch your heart in profound ways. They can bind you closer together and connect you to what truly matters. Young ones might help you find the magic in everyday miracles that you may otherwise look past. What a sacred honor to help your children expand into the fullness of their potential!

As a soulful couple, you can be a loving witness and well-wisher to your children. As parents, the rewards that you receive for your sacrifices are immeasurable. Throughout their development, your children can fill your hearts with great pride and gratitude. You make a significant difference by raising loving, competent adults who make their mark on this world.

TAKING ACTION

Personal Practice: Speaking Positively to Your Children

In your own words and manner, genuinely communicate affirming messages to your children and ask your spouse to do the same. Witness your child(ren)'s reactions to each of your positive comments. Discuss with your spouse what you are experiencing. What progress in attitude and behavior do you each notice over the span of a week? a month?

Soulful Connection: Clarifying a Parenting Concern

Sit close to each other and look into each other's eyes. Breathe slowly. Close your eyes and be present to your thoughts and feelings as you proceed with this exercise. Get in sync with each other to sustain your closeness as you address a challenging situation as a parent.

Internally name one issue or concern regarding your child or your conflicting parenting styles that you want to clarify, resolve, or address. Ask yourself, "How am I feeling right now?" Scan your body for sensations and cues to your emotions. Then consider, "What do I need now to find a solution, to complete something with someone, or to come to inner peace?"

Decide who speaks first about the issue you want to address, while the other one listens.

Speaker: "I want to talk to you about ... [specific situation]."

"I am feeling ... about ..." Take responsibility for what you feel in reaction to what happened. Use *I* messages, not accusatory *you* statements.

Listener: Acknowledge that you understand what your dear one is talking about. Ask a question only for clarification. Do not inject your own story or agenda into the conversation; just reflect back the crux of the message—the main content and feelings expressed.

Speaker: Continue when you feel understood and your partner is being an active listener. Share: "What I need right now is ..."

Listener: Help your beloved get a clear grasp of this situation. Formulate a plan of how to handle this concern, and similar ones, in the future. Create an agreement and write it down to remember.

Switch and do the same with the listener becoming the speaker, if time and energy permit. Otherwise, schedule another time to talk. Follow through as soon as possible.

Soulful Connection: Creating Parenting Agreements

Set aside an hour or more to talk about your parenting philosophies, needs, and expectations.

Brainstorm a collective list of what is most important in sustaining your soulful relationship while parenting your child(ren). Record the flow of ideas in writing without judgment or censorship. Then go back over the list and place an asterisk by the priorities. Once you feel good about your list, narrow it down to three or four key guidelines to remember. These may be items like speaking positively about each other, refraining from taking a child's side against the other parent, or asking for support when your emotions are triggered. Repeat them to each other, so you know that you have reached agreement and then celebrate!

You might want to maintain a growing list of ideas as you focus on this vital aspect of your marriage. Keep the dialogue alive and proactive.

Soulful Connection: Developing Spiritually

As an ongoing practice, discuss with your beloved what and how you want to teach your children about spiritual life. This may evolve over time as beliefs and circumstances change.

Here are some simple ways to help you cultivate your family's spiritual nature:

1. Visit your local library or bookstore. Find some books, movies, audiotapes, or CDs with themes such as morality, peace, and spiritual awareness from your religious background and others. Take time to experience them together and share your favorite parts.

2. To help your family relax at bedtime, practice various breathing techniques, such as this one: Inhale "I am." Exhale "calming." Repeat four or five times. Then say this simple visualization:

   "Imagine sitting on a hilltop watching a beautiful sunset. With each breath, the sun descends a bit more in the evening sky, as you slowly sink into deep sleep."

3. Share stories from your childhood of when God seemed close, or moments of spiritual awareness. Ask your beloved and your children to share their special spiritual experiences or beliefs about God (or whatever name you use), or angels, ghosts, spiritual energy, or magical or mystical awareness. Be open to learning and exploring together.

4. Develop rituals for you and your family to connect spiritually. Use prayers, songs, meditations, poems, healing techniques, and words of gratitude to nourish your souls and awaken your realization of the unity of all life.

5. Visit places of worship that reflect your shared beliefs as a couple. Encourage your child(ren) to set aside time and space for holiness and reverence.

6. Have a moment of silence or a prayer before meals and bedtime to provide a sacred atmosphere of peace. Share as a couple and family what you are grateful for and what you want to do to help others.

Vision for the Future

Expanding and Elevating Your Love

> The world we want for ourselves and our children
> will not emerge from electronic speed but rather
> from spiritual stillness that takes root in our souls.
> Then, and only then, will we create a world that
> reflects the heart instead of shattering it.
>
> —Marianne Williamson, *The Gift of Change: Spiritual Guidance*
> *for a Radically New Life*

Imagine that you and your sweetheart reside in an elegant, spacious mansion on a large estate. You emanate the splendor of a king and a queen. Your future is bright and hopeful. Your spirits soar as you picture all that is possible in the years to come.

As time goes by, you spend more of your time engaging in routine activities and conversations, occupying just a few relatively small rooms in your vast mansion. Have you been actively exploring the beauty and grandeur of your majestic palace? Perhaps you rarely visit your expansive, glorious garden. Your royal crowns are tucked away in a closet and your robes are getting tattered. You feel an inexplicable ache in your heart and wonder why.

Notice the clutter in your living space from the baggage you never bothered to unpack and put away. Are you longing to clear your pathways so that you can be more present in this moment, without tripping over the past, and design a future that allows you to explore the vast possibilities for you as individuals and the two of you together? Will you dare to declare it time to clean house, discover new relationship territory, and claim your birthright as royal residents of heaven on earth?

You and your beloved can serve as tour guides for each other of your expansive mansion of love that will continue your exciting adventure together well into the future. You can open doorways into aspects of yourself and aspects of your life together as a soulful couple that you might not realize exist. The map of the palace is tucked in the secret chambers of your heart. Discover the keys, venture into the hidden areas, unlock the doors, and luxuriate in the rooms of your soul. What a delightful treasure hunt!

Discover the Secret Keys to the Palace

Regarding each other as the king and queen of your world provides a strong foundation for mutual support as your personal transformations unfold. Look at each other and see the royal bearing. Delve into the heart of your majestic partner. Recognize her kindness, compassion, and nurturance. Acknowledge his strength, courage, and humility. As you slow down and heighten your awareness, you develop more skills to create and sustain your soulful relationship. These skills are the keys to your and your beloved's palace.

Actively taking good care of yourself is one key to elevating your love of life—and love life—beyond the fight-flight-freeze survival modes. One or both of you may decide to eat more healthfully, exercise more consistently, and get sufficient amounts of rest. These three lifestyle changes improve physical well-being and increase energy levels, so that you feel greater harmony in life.

Going beyond physical well-being, as you take more time to genuinely relax and focus on the present moment, you may experience flashes of inspiration, insight, and creativity. More joy, delight, and wonder might work their way into your heart! Use this intuitive sensitivity to connect soulfully with your beloved. For example, meditating together can bring you closer in your hearts, helping you awaken to the Unlimited Love of the Universe (a romantic name for God).

Another key to the palace is the ability to recognize old thought patterns and shift them so they better fit your life now. As you move from the conventional to the soulful point of view, you may feel the discomfort of being in the gap—the old way is not working but the new way is not yet established. Hang in there. Keep moving forward on your path, one step at a time.

Shift in Consciousness

Conventional Model: Partners Coexisting

I am a separate person from you. I do the best I can to get along with you and hope things work out okay. We each have our own way of doing things and we learn to accept and trust each other, so that we can live as life partners.

Soulful Model: Partners Spiritually Connecting

As I do my personal growth work and come to know more of my true essence, I realize I am soulfully connected to you and to all of life. I embrace you as a catalyst for my self-discovery and self-realization on my spiritual journey.

What does being soulful mean to you? Try using the letters as an acrostic to list words to describe *soulful*. Here is one example. What would you add?

Sacred

Open

Understanding

Loving

Fulfilling

Uplifting

Light

Share your acrostic with your partner. Allowing your hearts to connect and activating your warmth can help ease the way to being more soulful.

Just keep talking with your partner to understand where you are now and where you want to go on the spiritual path. What do you long for? What is your vision for your future? You can envision, plan, and build a glorious future together. Perhaps posting one of these acrostics in a visible location, such as your desktop, will serve as a guide to developing desired qualities for building your future.

Another key to the palace is tenacity—having the strength and the courage to keep at it. As you know, relationships move through stages and cycles. Having the keys to the palace means that you keep opening new gates to awareness, growth, and success in your journey as a soulful couple. Spirals of repeated patterns may show you issues that you need to resolve in yourself and in your relationship. Be aware that, in the difficult moments, you may get discouraged and want to give up. Take heart—you may need to shift your perspective about what is happening. Interpretations can be spun many different ways. Choose those that empower you. Be creative.

Shift in Consciousness

Conventional Model: Cut Your Losses

Good times seem like they will last forever. When things get stalled, old, broken, or undesirable, you get rid of them, like clothes, appliances, cars, homes ... and relationships. Routines and dull energy lead to boredom and lack of passion. When the relationship bogs down for a while, you believe that love is gone and think that the relationship is over.

Soulful Model: See the Cycle

You realize that your relationship, like all of life, is in a state of flux, with dynamic cycles and stages. You recognize and welcome cycles, avoid power struggles, and weather the storms. You strive to be aware, grateful, humble, vulnerable, and resilient. With understanding and resolve, you seek to make inroads into recurring issues. Progress, however small, is acknowledged. You do not readily quit.

Small Gestures, Big Future

Awaken from your trance of mundane living and treat your beloved as special and dear. Wash off your windows so you can see where you are and what lies ahead. You know how easy it is to take him for granted, blame her for little or big things, and ignore how he is doing. Take notice. Shift your focus to truly experience your dear one. Watch her as she goes about her daily routine. Study him as he takes care of things around the house. Warm your heart with gratitude and pleasure. Simple gestures can add more goodwill. Smiling, hugging, and looking into each other's eyes, for even a moment, creates connection and shows that you are open and receptive to love. This all clears the pathway to the future you desire.

Encourage your lover to discover and honor his uniqueness and to express his authentic self in the family and in all of life. Life can be so much sweeter when you regularly affirm and encourage each other. What if you make time to acknowledge each other's essence, core nature, character, and gifts on a daily or weekly basis? How much more honored you would each feel in your own home, as the king and the queen.

Being overjoyed at seeing each other can be a surprise that motivates you to pay more attention to each other. Although it is difficult to rival a dog's continual excitement in welcoming you home, warmly greet or at least acknowledge your mate when she comes home. This can greatly enhance your relationship. Spontaneous, genuine compliments, affectionate touching, pleasant surprises, and daily acts of serving each other show your appreciation. You can learn to be a sanctuary for each other.

Be a Sanctuary for Each Other: Ric and Robert

Together we travel the world in support and love, in respect, and with honor for each other. Like many others, early on, we fell into the trap that follows this basic formula: We meet, we love, we see who lies beneath the surface, we manipulate the other to re-create them in our own image. This does not work. Once we learned that we need not change each other, the relationship grew stronger, beyond our expectations, and allowed us to focus on and celebrate the very real person standing before us.

Let us not be tricked into thinking that we are two incomplete halves of a whole. We all enter our marriages as wonderfully unique individuals. Let us celebrate, promote, laugh, and accept that profoundly simple principle. Our partners are not our better halves! Think about what that implies about our own self-worth.

My partner and I come to the relationship complete in ourselves. Tread cautiously—if we look to our spouse to make us whole, we set him up for failure. Neither of us came to the relationship as half a person searching for our other half, a pot without a lid, somehow incomplete. Instead we've learned to stand as two individuals who have seen in each other a like-minded soul—someone who sees the world much as we do, someone whose most basic and fundamental values align with our own.

Your relationship truly lives in your own mind and heart—what is your inner conversation? Are you moaning and groaning about what she didn't do or blaming him for what he did do? What kind of future does that kind of resentment and bitterness bring? Instead, acknowledge your feelings, then shift to practicing loving-kindness. (See the Loving-Kindness Prayer, page 153.)

What if, beyond all the circumstances, moods, wounds, and joys, you realize that pure Love abounds? Visualize the expansive palace of your sacred relationship. Fling open the doors and windows so the fresh breeze of absolute unconditional acceptance wafts over you. Let that feeling deepen. Take a moment now to affirm in your heart how precious your beloved is to you. As you create your vision for your future, dare to think the unthinkable, imagine the unimaginable!

Revealing Your Golden Buddha

The more you focus on your own personal growth, attending to the neglected aspects of yourself, the more available you are to emanate love, harmony, and beauty. Being a powerful, peaceful source of inspiration for others is a way of contributing goodness to the world. The following true story of the golden Buddha can remind you of your own hidden treasures. Taking time to mine the gold brings you more profound gratitude and awe.

In order to build a Bangkok highway during 1957, a Thai monastery and its clay Buddha had to be relocated. The group of monks assigned to the task of hoisting the gigantic idol by crane noticed that its weight was causing it to crack. Then, as rain began falling, the head monk became very concerned about damage to the sacred Buddha. He ordered the statue to be lowered to the ground and covered with a large canvas tarp to protect it.

Inspecting the Buddha that evening, the head monk shone his flashlight under the tarp to make sure the figure was staying dry. As the light reached the crack, he was struck by a thin gleam shining back. Curious as to what might be underneath the clay, the monk fetched a chisel and hammer from the monastery and began knocking shards off the clay. Soon the light beam grew brighter and larger. After hours of intense labor, the monk was astonished to be facing an extraordinary solid-gold Buddha.

Historians speculate that a few hundred years before the head monk's discovery, Thailand (formerly Siam) was on the verge of being invaded by the Burmese army. Anticipating the attack, Siamese monks sought to protect their precious golden Buddha from looting by hiding it under a thick layer of clay. Because the Burmese slaughtered all the Siamese monks, the golden Buddha remained concealed for centuries.[1]

A powerful lesson can be gleaned from this story. Like the clay Buddha, consider that you are covered by a clay shell created from years of protective defenses, yet underneath lies your golden essence or true self. Your central life mission may be to rediscover your authentic nature. How exquisite it is for you and your beloved to spend years chiseling alongside one another.

Progressing on Your Path

Taking small steps daily in the direction you want to travel on your journey of being a soulful couple helps you make cumulative progress. Perhaps you would enjoy the bedtime ritual of reviewing your day, alone or with your partner, to recount what you are grateful for, what successes or accomplishments you have had, and what qualities you are developing. This can be a touchstone for clarity and courage to stay true to your path. Progressing on your path usually occurs gradually, in response to intention, commitment, and caring action. Keep correcting your course by making subtle shifts in your attitude, words, actions, or reactions.

Sometimes a drastic shift can happen in an instant and create a break-through that changes your life. One female friend shared that during the third year of marriage her husband grew weary of her recurrent dramatic episodes. When she threatened to commit suicide during an argument with her husband, the man called the police and had his wife confined to a psychiatric ward for a full week. During intensive group therapy, the woman developed sincere remorse for her pattern of histrionic behav-ior. When she returned home, she apologized to her husband and began to communicate honestly and clearly with him, for which he expressed strong appreciation. The couple has greatly enjoyed their relationship for the two years since the woman's hospitalization.

Remember that opportunities or crises may come at any time. Sometimes you may feel as if you are walking through the darkness, not sure of where you are or what is happening. How can you assess whether this change is in service to your development and to the growth of your relationship? Be wary of wild goose chases that take you further from where you are trying to go. Tell your truth and use your intuition or gut instinct. Be prepared to open the gifts life offers you.

If you and your mate can survive big changes and manage the daily challenges, your small efforts can yield cumulative results. You can accrue large dividends in your love fortune. Together you invest in each other, in love itself, in your future, and in the future for the next generations.

White Bird Must Fly: Jere and Regina

"White bird must fly, or she will die" was our theme song. This line, from the 1968 signature hit by the music group It's a Beautiful Day, may have been written about escaping a life of drudgery or confinement, but for my new husband Jere and me, who met in 1971 and married in 1973, it spoke to our mutual longing for the "highest spiritual realization." In those days we aimed that flight toward God, coming as we did from lives of religious service (Jere in the Catholic priesthood, me from the convent). Then, it meant that we celebrated the other's freedom to pursue the Path, whether that took us individually to India, or deeper into some social cause at home. Occasionally, we flew together. At other times, we suffered the loneliness of waiting in the nest. But the bottom line endured, often despite ourselves, as the winds of grace carried us! Again and again, we reviewed our commitment to witnessing the unfolding of another's soul attempting to achieve its fullest potential according to the Will of God.

Today, no longer so heavy with expectations, after forty years together we enter what Teilhard de Chardin called the stage of diminishment. Not a bad thing! We blessedly cry more easily. We acutely feel the pain when our words or deeds violate the compassion we've promised one another. We limp along, with fewer bursts of ecstatic flight, accepting life as it is. Now, with tentative wings, poised at the edge of the branch, we celebrate this moment with its clear promise—the loving and the letting go.

Loving beyond Death

At the end of your life, you certainly want to know, with peaceful clarity, that you made a difference in this world; that you lived fully and loved to the best of your ability. Knowing that you greatly enriched your spouse's life provides a sense of deep, rich contentment.

No one can absolutely know how the universe works. Mysteries of life and life after death abound. You may wonder whether your soul is reincarnated after death, whether you reunite with loved ones in other realms, whether you remember experiencing each other from past lives, or whether your souls arrange to meet again on the earthly plane. Many of you may have had supernatural glimpses into your soul's truth.

A Remarkable Woman Gives Gifts after Her Death: Brenda

A forty-six-year-old mother of four sons surprised her children, her husband, and his new fiancée with heartwarming holiday letters two years after her death from cancer.

As a parting gift, she entrusted a letter to an anonymous friend to deliver at the right time. The letter was addressed to a local radio station and contained two other letters—one for her husband and another for the new love of his life. The station grants wishes for a select few who send in letters. This remarkable woman's wishes were finally revealed two years later when the station brought her husband into the studio and read the note to him on air.

"When you are in receipt of this letter, I will have already lost my battle to ovarian cancer," the letter began. "I told [my friend] once my loving husband had moved on in his life and had met someone to share his life with again, to mail this letter to all of you at the station."

Her first wish to her recently engaged husband was a request for the station to give his new lifelong partner a pampering session. "She deserves it, being a stepmother to all those boys," the letter read. "Make her smile and know her efforts are truly appreciated by me. Thank you," she added. "I love you, whoever you are."

The second wish was a magical trip for the entire family to a place where they can "enjoy each other's company and companionship as a family and create those memories that will be with them forever."

The final wish was earmarked for the hospital doctors and nurses who took care of her while she was sick. She asked that they be given a "night out full of drinks, food, and fun for all they do every day for the cancer patients they encounter."

The station paired up with local businesses to help grant these three wishes, including sending the family of eight, which now incorporates the husband's two soon-to-be stepchildren, on a four-day vacation.

The radio host read the letter with a shaky voice to the loving husband, who was sitting flabbergasted in the station, wiping away his tears throughout. "Love survives long after the body is gone," commented the radio host.

My Spiritual Marriage: Christine

"You know I'm going first," he said, as he crawled into bed at midnight. "Stop it!" I replied. "You stand in front of our kids and say, 'What you fear, you create!'" He cuddled me up in his arms and hugged me tight. This would be the last night I would feel his arms this way.

My life changed in an instant the next morning. I got the call that most of us don't think will happen to us, even when it has crossed our minds. We push it out like any negative thought we don't want to be true. And yet for some of us, it becomes our reality.

Tom, my beautiful, sweet, joyful husband of twenty-nine years, walked off our porch to drive to the airport. At the corner of a highway he had driven hundreds of times, he lost control of his car. It rolled over two and a half times, and he suffered massive, fatal head injuries. Thirteen days later, he saved five lives and more by donating his organs.

We never talked with words again yet we have shared countless thoughts, conversations, and experiences that are as real as if he were physically still with me. I do admit, I miss his physical touch but he does touch me! It's been almost seven years and we remain very present with each other.

The night they transplanted his heart and four other major organs, Tom let me know just how thin the veil is by bringing me into the white light. He lit the room, our sleeping son and me, bringing us into his energy. And we had the last real conversation. That's when I knew for sure ... there is no separation. BELIEVE![2]

Hopefully, these two stories expand your faith and inspire you to consider the possibilities for lasting rich connections with your beloved beyond this life. Do you have the desire to discuss death and dying with your spouse? Books, clergy, and seminars are valuable resources to help you cope with end-of-life concerns. Planning your own eulogy and memorial service can be a powerful experience that helps clarify what is truly important to you. How do you want to be remembered?

A friend's husband died and she missed him terribly. Several weeks after his death, she awoke nightly to a startling image of a pair of hands on the ceiling. Perplexed, she called out, "Fred, is that you?" She was too grief-stricken to be certain of the answer. A few weeks later, she received a strange call from a long-lost acquaintance. "I know this sounds really weird, especially since I haven't seen you in years. But for the last few weeks I have had a dream in which Fred comes to me and says to tell you that the handprints on the ceiling are his. Does that mean anything to you?" Amazing, right?

A Powerful Ripple Effect

Life is full of mystery. You each have your own unique version of reality. Being daring enough to be true to yourself is an inspiration to all who know you or know of you, even if they do not agree with you all the time. Whether or not you realize it, others are watching you, modeling your behavior, and absorbing the love and harmony you exude. Perhaps a stranger sees your graceful ways of handling a difficult situation at work or in a public setting. Maybe someone is touched by something you said in passing.

You just never know how many people you affect. Do you still remember certain words of wisdom spoken by a coach, a college professor, or a schoolteacher? Sometimes a new perspective or an aha moment can come from a conversation, a blog, a media post, or a letter. Something a character says on a television show or in a movie can change the course of your life. Messages come in many different forms. Be receptive. Also, be conscious of the messages that you continually broadcast, many of which ripple out to countless others, including your partner.

Sharing your life in a sacred relationship with your partner extends out to all those you influence. In your own circle of influence, when you and your partner are cherishing each other, your family and friends enjoy your company. They celebrate your joy, have compassion for your struggles, and are attracted to being with you. You open the pathways for others to enjoy more intimacy and soulfulness by your example.

The peacefulness in your house is palpable to those who enter your home. As you expand the capacity for greater peace in your heart, all who come in contact with you can experience serenity. Even those you reach in virtual forums or who know of you through others can benefit from the work you do for your personal growth. On a spiritual level, your impact may be far greater than you can know.

Imagine your children or other relatives growing up, creating sacred unions, and raising their own soulful children. Following your example, they revere the flame of love that you have transmitted to them. This is your legacy.

Picture yourself at the end of your life, fulfilled, satisfied, complete, whole, at peace. As you visualize looking in the mirror, you witness your advanced, evolved self. Take an inner snapshot. Use this clear image as your guide, like a mentor, coach, elder, or wise one. Stay open to knowing and becoming this person.

Empower your dreams, hopes, goals, time lines, and next steps for your relationship. Create a vision board using magazine graphics, photos, and words showing the qualities, activities, people, and places that you want to call forth or engage with during the coming year.

Identify your own secrets for refreshing, enlivening, and balancing your relationship. You and your sweetheart have the potential to ultimately paint a masterpiece together—your unique sacred marriage!

Your hearts are a portal to the Divine, to the Infinite. Let Love and Light shine!

TAKING ACTION

Soulful Connection: Visiting Your Palace

For a fun in-house date night, experiment with this visualization and conversation.

Take a few moments to relax your body, breathe deeply, and quiet your mind. Alternate telling each other about a room in the palace of your relationship that you have enjoyed exploring together. What might make it even more exciting or meaningful for you in the future? Be descriptive or colorful in your depictions. For example: Tell your beloved how much you enjoy going on cultural outings, like music concerts, art galleries, or dance revues. How could you bring more of the arts into your palace?

Detail some of the pleasures that you recall on vacations; suggest an exotic location that you would be thrilled to visit. Research and plan a future trip together. You might relate how close you feel toward your spouse when you pray together and that you would love to engage in more spiritual practice. Perhaps you want to visit some churches or places of worship, or set up your own meditation area in your home. Specify what you enjoy during lovemaking and what would further gratify you. Offer fresh possibilities in the form of What if ...? Take turns sharing. Be creative and proactive. Be sure to follow through on your plans. Empower positive actions so you build trust in yourselves and in each other to create the future you desire.

Soulful Connection: Healing Mantra

Take ten minutes of quiet time together to practice the traditional Hawaiian healing mantra, which has become widespread in recent years. This mantra, called *ho'oponopono* (to make right), consists of four simple yet heartfelt sentences. Focus on something that seems unresolved between you as you say the whole sequence to each other slowly. Let the emotions surface. Allow the basic truth to permeate your heart and soul.

I'm sorry.

Please forgive me.

Thank you.

I love you.

You can use this healing mantra internally, secretly, directed toward your partner. Notice what happens to your relationship. Choosing to elevate your awareness is a blessing. You may experience more synergy and cooperation by treating each other as complete and whole. Preserving your own values, needs, and interests while harmoniously collaborating with your partner makes for a wonderful dream come true.

Personal Practice: Loving-Kindness Prayer

You can practice this loving-kindness prayer to enhance your good feelings toward your partner.

Begin by bringing to mind someone it is easy to feel loving-kindness toward—someone from the past or present, perhaps a child or a pet. Choose an easy, simple relationship at first.

Allow yourself to hold her in your awareness, perhaps seeing her in your mind's eye or feeling her essence in your heart. Can you feel a sense of loving-kindness toward her? As you hold her in your awareness, begin to send wishes of loving-kindness to her.

Silently repeat these phrases:

May you be safe.

May you be happy.

May you be healthy.

May you live with ease.

Focusing on yourself, and cradling the sense of yourself in your awareness, repeat these words silently:

May I be safe.

May I be happy.

May I be healthy.

May I live with ease.

Maybe to you it feels artificial and stilted to say such things to yourself, for yourself, or maybe you're not feeling loving-kindness at this moment—that's okay. Whatever you're feeling, you can hold the intention of loving-kindness, offering it from wherever you are, however you are now.

Take a few deep breaths and practice once more, this time focusing on your beloved partner:

May you be safe.

May you be happy.

May you be healthy.

May you live with ease.

Sending the loving-kindness blessing to yourself, your partner, and others in your life can be very humbling and powerful. Also, send the blessing to areas of the world or situations that need healing. If you dare, send the loving-kindness prayer to someone you have great difficulty getting along with or even someone who has passed on, with whom you have unfinished business. You may never know the effect of this practice on others, but you can be sure it will soften your own heart and help you be more loving and kind.

Soulful Connection: Bring Your Dreams and Goals to Life

In this activity, you activate a mind movie in your imagination of the future you want to create. Take turns doing this exercise with your partner, either indoors or outside. Allow twenty to thirty minutes to complete the process. Use your journal to record your awarenesses or realizations. Notice what happens in the next months or years as a result of doing this exercise.

Choose who goes first in moving toward your goals (#1) and who poses as your obstacles and acts as your facilitator (#2).

#1: Stand upright, with your feet grounded in the earth and your head straight. Breathe and relax. Look straight ahead at a blank wall about ten to twenty feet away (or at a tree or a structure in your yard). Project onto the wall your mind movie of where you are progressing in your future. Imagine

your dreams and goals having been realized. Notice your personal qualities, attitudes, actions, and lifestyle. Walk toward the blank wall, as if you
were entering the movie. When you get to the wall (tree, or structure), stop
for a minute and savor how wonderful you feel. Ah. Now walk back to your
original spot and assume the beginning posture—standing upright, with
your feet grounded in the earth and your head straight.

#2: Stand between #1 and the vision of her future. Position yourself
about ten feet from #1, at a right angle with your arm outstretched to block
the path of #1. This is #2 posing as the obstacles to #1 reaching her goals.
Those obstacles could be fears, doubts, feelings of inadequacy, or patterns
of avoidance, such as procrastination or making excuses.

#1: Walk toward your partner's outstretched arm, which is blocking your
progress along your path until you actually make contact with #2's arm. Feel
what it is like to physically hit the obstacle. What do you notice emotionally? Return to your original spot and beginning posture.

#2: Be a facilitator by reminding #1 of the flight pattern of thoughts,
feelings, or behaviors that prevent her from progressing toward her goals.

#1: Walk forward again to your partner's arm as your obstacle. Look
ahead at the mind movie of your fulfilling life. How do you feel? How is
your energy?

#1: Go back to the original spot and beginning posture, relax, and re-
lease the flight reaction.

#2: Remind her of her fight patterns. "You are clear about what you want
out of life and you won't be stopped." Snap your fingers in front of her fore-
head to activate the drive to forge ahead.

#1: Move toward your partner's arm, representing your obstacle. Keep
your focus on your dreams and goals. Observe your thoughts, actions, and
feelings. Return to the original spot and to your beginning posture.

#2: Tell your partner to feel the power of her determination. "The vision
on the wall ahead is your birthright, the natural fulfillment of the seeds of
potential planted in your soul. It is yours. Go to it." Activate the power in her
gut by snapping your fingers in front of #1's belly. "Go forth and blossom,
as you are meant to do."

#1: Walk toward your goals, meeting your obstacles and noticing what
happens as you resolutely move forward toward your dreams.

Share your experience and insights with your partner. Then switch roles.

You may want to remember your mind movie by writing down the details in your journal, making a collage of printed images or photographs, or making an audio recording to replay at future times. Be sure to speak in the first person, present tense, when you voice affirmations and positive statements. This sets up new mental pathways to your future. You can say things like these: "I am taking small steps daily to make a wonderful future for my family and me." "I am getting stronger, clearer, more courageous, and more loving each day." "My career is unfolding as it should. I am proud of my accomplishments and my successes." "I love my wife and children more and more each day."

Have fun with positive, life-affirming statements. Be sure to say what is true for you. You do not want to make statements that exaggerate or distort where you are today. This may cause inner conflict because the words are too far from your current reality. Be willing to bring your mind movie to fruition, and be open to manifesting something even better than what you envisioned.

Personal Practice: Pillar of Light and Breath

Some people say that we live in a call-and-response universe. As you call out for fulfillment, the Universe responds with what ultimately serves you, although you do not always receive what you think you want. Your openness and vulnerability correlate with your level of faith and trust. If you feel the need to be in control of everything, the energy to reach your path may be blocked. Release the tight hold on your agenda and witness what happens. In this activity, take time to be receptive so that you can more readily perceive the wisdom of your soul.

> It is not the solid wood that can become a flute, it is the empty reed.
>
> —Hazrat Inayat Khan, *Bowl of Saki*

Sit quietly, without distractions, with your spine straight and your feet on the ground. When you are relaxed and receptive, imagine a beam of light coming down through the top of your head, through your body, and exiting through the soles of your feet. Then picture a wave of energy rising up from the ground, filling you to the top of your head and flowing up into the sky.

Include your breath in the visualization. Inhale, letting the breath rise from the earth to the top of your head, then exhale up to the sky. Now, inhale from the sky and exhale down into the earth. Repeat this sequence five times. Feel the energy that you have activated.

Continue your meditation by becoming as still and receptive as possible. Ask for divine guidance and discerning wisdom to carry out what truly serves you and your world. Use your journal or talk with your partner or coach about such questions as:

What do you see when you view your life from the soul's perspective?

How do you want your world to appear?

What aspect of your life is currently aligned with your higher purpose?

What aspects of your inner or outer life are out of alignment?

What if you and your partner could actually co-create your lives to harmonize with your soul purposes?

As you become clearer about your purpose, you may feel the desire to extend yourself beyond that purpose. Maybe you feel the desire or calling to serve more, both in terms of quality action and the number of people you touch. You naturally attract the right people and opportunities to fulfill your purpose when your drive is strong enough.

The Promise of Love

Many people live as human beings seeking spiritual experiences. What if you live as a spiritual being having a human experience?

Deep in your heart and soul you have connected with your beloved. You delight in her smile, his voice, the delectable smell of your beloved's skin and hair. You cannot get enough of each other. Each day is filled with magical moments and delicious treats of love. Your spirit soars! Wow, this is really happening! You have found your true love, the one with whom you'll spend the rest of your life learning and growing, sharing hardships, triumphs, and special secrets. You feel wonderfully accepted for who you are. You sense that nothing can change this feeling; it will endure forever.

The many facets of being together become more intense than you ever imagined. The heights are higher, the depths are deeper. You finally feel the freedom to be yourself *and* to be loved. Ah, what a relief! The doors and windows of your soul are flying open and love abounds! The pink cloud of bliss makes everything so beautiful.

You connect on many levels; so much clicks with the two of you. The promise of love is alluring! You have decided to commit to each other, to marry, in excited anticipation of living with your best friend and having love that lasts a lifetime. You hope to grow old together, to come to know, love, and trust each other through all circumstances.

But day-to-day reality soon sets in. Along with relishing the magic moments, you become starkly aware of how demanding your lives can be. Your mutual mundane responsibilities begin to intrude. Over the years, your lives fill with jobs, budgeting, household chores, parenting, health concerns, disappointments, and so forth. The romantic feelings that you often share with one another may frequently seem buried under the busy-ness, challenges, and adversities of daily living.

Handling the everyday tasks and demands, along with cultivating your relationship, can make you feel as if you are in a pressure cooker. When the heat is turned up, you wonder how you are going to manage. So much is happening at once that you may become off-center. Fatigued and irritable, you ponder what went wrong. Dwelling on your partner's personality flaws and quirks, you may become confused, disappointed, withdrawn, angry, perhaps judgmental—you know the list. You are trying hard to continue to love your mate, yet this seems increasingly difficult. Your buttons get pushed; you push your partner's buttons. This pattern of behavior sucks the joy out of the present moment. At times, judging and blaming your partner seems so justified that it's scary.

In quiet moments, you may sense a restless, unnamable dissatisfaction rumbling deep inside you. Something is not right. In the face of burdensome routines and of having your deficiencies and idiosyncrasies exposed, you may question whether you can handle the stress and emotions. Also, you might seriously question whether your relationship can flourish. The solemn inner voice whispers, "Do I really want to pull away from my partner?" The promise of enduring love certainly seems to be falling short.

Every couple seems to go through these cycles of coming together and pulling apart. It is the natural ebb and flow of marriage. In this book you have learned attitudes, skills, and action steps that guide you to new agreements and commitments to navigate these tides. You have learned the importance of increasing your awareness, forgiving yourself and your partner, taking the time to decide what is essential, following up with action steps, lending support.[1]

As you give loving attention to your own personal growth, tension between you and your partner subsides and you can more readily express and exchange your love. The promise of love becomes more palpable.

As you develop more sensitivity and compassion toward each other's needs, feelings, thoughts, beliefs, and hurts, you become more at ease with being unified *and* being separate. Hopefully, you become more graceful in the dance steps of partnership. The old struggles subside and your love flourishes.

As your essential self evolves and expands, you discover more of your life purpose. Imagine your marriage as a holy crucible—a healing vessel—that allows you to sanctify your union and provides the opportunity to release barriers to love. You can burn up the old, limiting patterns in the holy container of your marriage. Visualize being able to free yourself to truly love your partner in the most fulfilling and delicious ways!

How can you stay aware and awake to fulfill your life purpose? This is a tall order, especially in a culture that prizes busyness, where people are striving to do more and acquire more possessions. Perhaps you feel resigned at a core level that life is just about surviving. Perhaps you are not feeling supported to truly thrive. Is your partner your well-wisher, who wants you to become all you can be? Are you devoted to your partner's happiness and realization of his potential?

You can look at your life as a structure with supportive pillars. Those pillars might be commitment, passion, integrity, communication—ideals you strive for and use as touchstones to support your life decisions. What are yours? Take a few moments to jot down or discuss your ideas.

Set your intention to honor the spiritual awakening that you may be experiencing. Entertain the possibility that your marriage is arranged by a magnificent power of intelligence and love in the Universe. Your own soul or your sense of God may be manifesting just what you need to satisfy what you came to earth to fulfill. By being with someone who can help you heal old wounds, release restrictive patterns, and alter limiting beliefs, you and your beloved can free energy to satisfy your personal and combined goals. As you continue to do so, you increasingly thrive as a soulful couple.

Are you committed to moving toward achieving your love purpose(s)—what you are called to fulfill? Each of you has seeds of potential planted in your soul that this life can nurture and grow. You can engage in the process of awakening to your true purpose in being here. Will you include your partner in this intimate process?

Love can be like the bright, hot sun. Just as the sun radiates its illuminating warmth through its rays, your love reaches out into every aspect of your life. The more you infuse your life with love, the more you enrich yourself and others. Love is the central force field in the universe that makes life worthwhile, meaningful, and beautiful.

TAKING ACTION

Personal Practice and Soulful Connection: Feel the Energy

Make a date with your partner to engage in these energy exercises.

Sit or stand with your own palms facing each other. Rub your palms together and start to build up warmth. Then pull your hands apart slowly and feel the body's subtle energy. Imagine that you are forming a ball of this energy between your palms. Roll the ball around; make it bigger and smaller. If you are with your partner, combine your "balls of energy" to make a more potent one. Play with the energy and see what happens!

Soulful Connection:
Energy Bubble—Sharing Your Sacred Space

Take a moment to calm and center yourself, so that you can feel your feet on the ground. Breathe calmly. Stand facing each other. Ask your partner to walk toward you. Tell him when he has entered your personal space, your "energy bubble." Ask your mate to step out of your bubble, then back into it. Feel the edges of your personal energy field. Now you step into her bubble and out.

One of you may have a larger energy bubble than the other—and that is just fine. Notice where the seemingly separate selves are and where your energy fields overlap.

Make an agreement to honor each other's sense of personal space. Give permission to say when you feel as if your personal space is being invaded or violated in any way. Learn to realize when you are merging your energies in unhealthy ways, so that you can change these subtle patterns. Using the awareness of the energy bubble, you can learn to respect and honor each other's separate uniqueness.

Feeling centered and calm, turn your attention to your heart now. Recognize that your heart is centered between the earth and sky energies.

Awakening the heart's potential for love is at the center of sacred relation-ship. Focus on your heart-center. What love qualities are you developing in your relationship now? Enhancing these qualities gives life more meaning and dimension.

Soulful Connection: Being a Soulful Couple

Spend thirty to sixty minutes in a focused dialogue about being a soulful couple. Pick one or more of these topics to discuss, for the purpose of get-ting to know each other more intimately.

1. What does being a soulful couple mean to you? For example, we are a couple devoted to bringing more love into the world.

2. Identify and affirm what you are choosing to place at the center of your life. You each may have a different focus. For example: Is it being a kind person, caring for your family, becoming more spiritually fulfilled, serving others through your work or through community involvement?

3. Verbalize what truly matters to you and how to fuel the manifestation of your central values.

4. Share a few secrets in your heart about your life purpose.

Personal Practice: House of Love

Relax and let your imagination have some time and space. Imagine your relationship as a home for love. As in building a physical house, you need a strong foundation (your lower self, based on survival). See yourself func-tioning well on the everyday stuff-to-do realm.

Now picture your home, rising up on the pillars, with more floors. This is where your higher self can gain mastery and manifest your dreams and goals. What other rooms can you imagine? Places for playing, dancing, art, music? Your love chamber? Sacred meditation and prayer rooms? Expan-sive or cozy spaces for having fun and engaging in educational activities?

Integrating the realms of the lower self (earthbound, programmed) *and* the higher self (sky-aspiring, potential-oriented) can create a powerful bal-ance in your life structure—your mansion of love!

Notes

Chapter 2

1. Shelley Taylor, *The Tending Instinct: How Nurturing Is Essential to Who We Are and How We Live* (New York: Holt, 2002).
2. John Lennon, *In His Own Write* (New York: Simon and Schuster, 2000).
3. The AFDA Model, delineated in Ruth Sharon and Linda Clark, *Conflict: A Way to Peace—The AFDA Model* (Englewood, CO: The AFDA Group, Inc., 1989).
4. One kind of energy-clearing therapy is known as Emotional Freedom Techniques (EFT), a form of psychological acupressure based on the same energy meridians used in traditional acupuncture.

Chapter 3

1. If you are interested in learning more about personalities and styles, you can research systems such as the Enneagram, Myers-Briggs Type Indicator (MBTI), Neuro-Linguistics Programming (NLP), as well as love languages.
2. Ruth Sharon and Linda Clark, *Conflict: A Way to Peace—The AFDA Model* (Englewood, CO: The AFDA Group, Inc., 1989).

Chapter 4

1. Refer to the Fair Fighting guidelines in chapter 3 for ways to resolve conflicts and build your relationship.
2. Gary Chapman, *The Five Love Languages: How to Express Heartfelt Commitment to Your Mate* (Chicago: Northfield Publishing, 2004).
3. Roderick MacFarlane, "Never Listed His Faults," *Reader's Digest*, December 1992, 104.

Chapter 8

1. Jack Canfield and Mark Victor Hansen, *Chicken Soup for the Soul: 101 Stories to Open the Heart and Rekindle the Spirit* (Deerfield Beach, FL: Health Communications, 1993), 68–70.
2. From the unpublished short story "A Matter of the Heart: One Woman's Journey through Grief and Beyond" by Christine Berry, © 2008. Used with permission.

Invitation

1. The AFDA Model, as delineated in Ruth Sharon and Linda Clark, *Conflict: A Way to Peace—The AFDA Model* (Englewood, CO: The AFDA Group, Inc., 1989).

Suggestions for Further Reading

Alex, Janelle and Rob. *Inspired Couples in Business and in Love*. Create Space, 2014.

Apple, Mali, and Joe Dunn. *The Soulmate Experience: A Practical Guide to Creating Extraordinary Relationships*. San Rafael, CA: A Higher Possibility, 2011.

Gottman, John, and Nan Silver. *The Seven Principles for Making Marriage Work: A Practical Guide from the Foremost Relationship Expert*. New York: Three River Press, 1999.

———. *What Makes Love Last? How to Build Trust and Avoid Betrayal*. New York: Simon and Schuster, 2012.

Hendricks, Gay and Kathlyn. *Conscious Loving: The Journey to Co-commitment*. New York: Bantam Books, 1992.

Hendrix, Harville. *Getting the Love You Want: A Guide for Couples*. New York: Henry Holt, 1988.

Hendrix, Harville, and Helen LaKelly Hunt. *Making Marriage Simple: 10 Relationship Solving Truths*. New York: Crown, 2013.

Johnson, Sue. *Hold Me Tight: Seven Conversations for a Lifetime of Love*. Boston: Shambhala, 2002.

McKay, Matthew, Patrick Fanning, and Kim Paleg. *Couple Skills: Making Your Relationship Work*. Oakland, CA: New Harbinger, 2006.

Moore, Thomas. *Soul Mates: Honoring the Mysteries of Love and Relationships*. New York: HarperCollins, 1994.

Real, Terrence. *The New Rules of Marriage: What You Need to Know to Make Your Love Work*. New York: Ballantine Books, 2007.

Richo, David. *How to Be an Adult in Relationships: The Five Keys to Mindful Loving*. Boston: Shambhala, 2002.

Schnarch, David. *Passionate Marriage: Love, Sex and Intimacy in Emotionally Committed Relationships*. New York: W.W. Norton, 1997.

Yerkavich, Milan and Kay. *How We Love: Discovering Your Love Style, Enhancing Your Marriage*. New York: Random House, 2008.

Inspiration

The Rebirthing of God
Christianity's Struggle for New Beginnings
By John Philip Newell

Drawing on modern prophets from East and West, and using the holy island of Iona as an icon of new beginnings, Celtic poet, peacemaker and scholar John Philip Newell dares us to imagine a new birth from deep within Christianity, a fresh stirring of the Spirit.

6 x 9, 160 pp, HC, 978-1-59473-542-4 **$19.99**

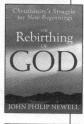

Finding God Beyond Religion: A Guide for Skeptics, Agnostics & Unorthodox Believers Inside & Outside the Church
By Tom Stella; Foreword by The Rev. Canon Marianne Wells Borg

Reinterprets traditional religious teachings central to the Christian faith for people who have outgrown the beliefs and devotional practices that once made sense to them.

6 x 9, 160 pp, Quality PB, 978-1-59473-485-4 **$16.99**

Fully Awake and Truly Alive: Spiritual Practices to Nurture Your Soul
By Rev. Jane E. Vennard; Foreword by Rami Shapiro

Illustrates the joys and frustrations of spiritual practice, offers insights from various religious traditions and provides exercises and meditations to help us become more fully alive.

6 x 9, 208 pp, Quality PB, 978-1-59473-473-1 **$16.99**

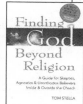

Journeys of Simplicity: Traveling Light with Thomas Merton, Bashō, Edward Abbey, Annie Dillard & Others *By Philip Harnden*

Invites you to consider a more graceful way of traveling through life. PB includes journal pages to help you get started on your own spiritual journey.

5 x 7¼, 144 pp, Quality PB, 978-1-59473-181-5 **$12.99**
5 x 7¼, 128 pp, HC, 978-1-893361-76-8 **$16.95**

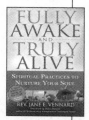

Perennial Wisdom for the Spiritually Independent
Sacred Teachings—Annotated & Explained
Annotation by Rami Shapiro; Foreword by Richard Rohr

Weaves sacred texts and teachings from the world's major religions into a coherent exploration of the five core questions at the heart of every religion's search.

5½ x 8½, 336 pp, Quality PB Original, 978-1-59473-515-8 **$16.99**

Saving Civility: 52 Ways to Tame Rude, Crude & Attitude for a Polite Planet
By Sara Hacala

Provides fifty-two practical ways you can reverse the course of incivility and make the world a more enriching, pleasant place to live.

6 x 9, 240 pp, Quality PB, 978-1-59473-314-7 **$16.99**

Spiritually Healthy Divorce: Navigating Disruption with Insight & Hope
By Carolyne Call

A spiritual map to help you move through the twists and turns of divorce.

6 x 9, 224 pp, Quality PB, 978-1-59473-288-1 **$16.99**

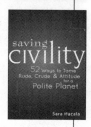

Or phone, fax, mail or email to: SKYLIGHT PATHS Publishing
Sunset Farm Offices, Route 4 • P.O. Box 237 • Woodstock, Vermont 05091
Tel: (802) 457-4000 • Fax: (802) 457-4004 • www.skylightpaths.com
Credit card orders: (800) 962-4544 (8:30AM–5:30PM EST Monday–Friday)
Generous discounts on quantity orders. SATISFACTION GUARANTEED. Prices subject to change.

Children's Spirituality

Remembering My Grandparent: A Kid's Own Grief Workbook in the Christian Tradition *By Nechama Liss-Levinson, PhD, and Rev. Molly Phinney Baskette, MDiv* 8 x 10, 48 pp, 2-color text, HC, 978-1-59473-212-6 **$16.99** *For ages 7 & up*

Does God Ever Sleep? *By Joan Sauro, CSJ*
A charming nighttime reminder that God is always present in our lives.
10 x 8½, 32 pp, Full-color photos, Quality PB, 978-1-59473-110-5 **$8.99** *For ages 3–6*

Does God Forgive Me? *By August Gold; Full-color photos by Diane Hardy Waller*
Gently shows how God forgives all that we do if we are truly sorry.
10 x 8½, 32 pp, Full-color photos, Quality PB, 978-1-59473-142-6 **$8.99** *For ages 3–6*

God Said Amen *By Sandy Eisenberg Sasso; Full-color illus. by Avi Katz*
A warm and inspiring tale that shows us that we need only reach out to each other to find the answers to our prayers.
9 x 12, 32 pp, Full-color illus., HC, 978-1-58023-080-3 **$16.95*** *For ages 4 & up*

How Does God Listen? *By Kay Lindahl; Full-color photos by Cynthia Maloney*
How do we know when God is listening to us? Children will find the answers to these questions as they engage their senses while the story unfolds, learning how God listens in the wind, waves, clouds, hot chocolate, perfume, our tears and our laughter.
10 x 8½, 32 pp, Full-color photos, Quality PB, 978-1-59473-084-9 **$8.99** *For ages 3–6*

In God's Hands *By Lawrence Kushner and Gary Schmidt; Full-color illus. by Matthew J. Baek*
A delightful, timeless legend that tells of the ordinary miracles that occur when we really, truly open our eyes to the world around us.
9 x 12, 32 pp, Full-color illus., HC, 978-1-58023-224-1 **$16.99*** *For ages 5 & up*

In God's Name *By Sandy Eisenberg Sasso; Full-color illus. by Phoebe Stone*
Like an ancient myth in its poetic text and vibrant illustrations, this award-winning modern fable about the search for God's name celebrates the diversity and, at the same time, the unity of all the people of the world.
9 x 12, 32 pp, Full-color illus., HC, 978-1-879045-26-2 **$16.99*** *For ages 4 & up*

Also available in Spanish: **El nombre de Dios**
9 x 12, 32 pp, Full-color illus., HC, 978-1-893361-63-8 **$16.95**

In Our Image: God's First Creatures
By Nancy Sohn Swartz; Full-color illus. by Melanie Hall
A playful new twist on the Genesis story—from the perspective of the animals. Celebrates the interconnectedness of nature and the harmony of all living things.
9 x 12, 32 pp, Full-color illus., HC, 978-1-879045-99-6 **$16.95*** *For ages 4 & up*
Animated app available on Apple App Store and the Google Play marketplace **$9.99**

Noah's Wife: The Story of Naamah
By Sandy Eisenberg Sasso; Full-color illus. by Bethanne Andersen
Opens young readers' religious imaginations to new ideas about the well-known story of the Flood. When God tells Noah to bring the animals of the world onto the ark, God also calls on Naamah, Noah's wife, to save each plant on Earth.
9 x 12, 32 pp, Full-color illus., HC, 978-1-58023-134-3 **$16.95*** *For ages 4 & up*

Also available: **Naamah:** Noah's Wife (A Board Book)
By Sandy Eisenberg Sasso; Full-color illus. by Bethanne Andersen
5 x 5, 24 pp, Full-color illus., Board Book, 978-1-893361-56-0 **$7.95** *For ages 1–4*

Where Does God Live? *By August Gold and Matthew J. Perlman*
Helps children and their parents find God in the world around us with simple, practical examples children can relate to.
10 x 8½, 32 pp, Full-color photos, Quality PB, 978-1-893361-39-3 **$8.99** *For ages 3–6*

* A book from Jewish Lights, SkyLight Paths' sister imprint

Judaism / Christianity / Islam / Interfaith

Sacred Laughter of the Sufis: Awakening the Soul with the Mulla's Comic Teaching Stories & Other Islamic Wisdom
By Imam Jamal Rahman
The legendary wisdom stories of Islam's great comic foil with spiritual insights for seekers of all traditions—or none. Connects the Mulla's stories to the issues at the heart of the spiritual quest.
6 x 9, 192 pp, Quality PB, 978-1-59473-547-9 **$16.99**

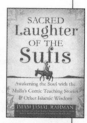

Spiritual Gems of Islam: Insights & Practices from the Qur'an, Hadith, Rumi & Muslim Teaching Stories to Enlighten the Heart & Mind
By Imam Jamal Rahman
Invites you—no matter what your practice may be—to access the treasure chest of Islamic spirituality and use its wealth in your own journey.
6 x 9, 256 pp, Quality PB, 978-1-59473-430-4 **$16.99**

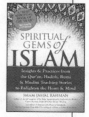

Religion Gone Astray: What We Found at the Heart of Interfaith
By Pastor Don Mackenzie, Rabbi Ted Falcon and Imam Jamal Rahman
Welcome to the deeper dimensions of interfaith dialogue—exploring that which divides us personally, spiritually and institutionally.
6 x 9, 192 pp, Quality PB, 978-1-59473-317-8 **$16.99**

Getting to the Heart of Interfaith: The Eye-Opening, Hope-Filled Friendship of a Pastor, a Rabbi & an Imam *By Pastor Don Mackenzie, Rabbi Ted Falcon and Imam Jamal Rahman*
6 x 9, 192 pp, Quality PB, 978-1-59473-263-8 **$16.99**

Hearing the Call across Traditions: Readings on Faith and Service
Edited by Adam Davis; Foreword by Eboo Patel
6 x 9, 352 pp, Quality PB, 978-1-59473-303-1 **$18.99**

How to Do Good & Avoid Evil: A Global Ethic from the Sources of Judaism
By Hans Küng and Rabbi Walter Homolka; Translated by Rev. Dr. John Bowden
6 x 9, 224 pp, HC, 978-1-59473-255-3 **$19.99**

All Politics Is Religious: Speaking Faith to the Media, Policy Makers and Community
By Rabbi Dennis S. Ross; Foreword by Rev. Barry W. Lynn
6 x 9, 192 pp, Quality PB, 978-1-59473-374-1 **$18.99**

Blessed Relief: What Christians Can Learn from Buddhists about Suffering
By Gordon Peerman 6 x 9, 208 pp, Quality PB, 978-1-59473-252-2 **$16.99**

Christians & Jews—Faith to Faith: Tragic History, Promising Present, Fragile Future *By Rabbi James Rudin*
6 x 9, 288 pp, HC, 978-1-58023-432-0 **$24.99***   Quality PB, 978-1-58023-717-8 **$18.99***

Christians & Jews in Dialogue: Learning in the Presence of the Other *By Mary C. Boys and Sara S. Lee; Foreword by Dorothy C. Bass* 6 x 9, 240 pp, Quality PB, 978-1-59473-254-6 **$18.99**

InterActive Faith: The Essential Interreligious Community-Building Handbook
Edited by Rev. Bud Heckman with Rori Picker Neiss; Foreword by Rev. Dirk Ficca
6 x 9, 304 pp, Quality PB, 978-1-59473-273-7 **$16.99**; HC, 978-1-59473-237-9 **$29.99**

The Jewish Approach to God: A Brief Introduction for Christians
By Rabbi Neil Gillman, PhD 5½ x 8½, 192 pp, Quality PB, 978-1-58023-190-9 **$16.95***

The Jewish Approach to Repairing the World (*Tikkun Olam*): A Brief Introduction for Christians *By Rabbi Elliot N. Dorff, PhD, with Rev. Cory Willson*
5½ x 8½, 256 pp, Quality PB, 978-1-58023-349-1 **$16.99***

The Jewish Connection to Israel, the Promised Land: A Brief Introduction for Christians *By Rabbi Eugene Korn, PhD* 5½ x 8½, 192 pp, Quality PB, 978-1-58023-318-7 **$14.99***

Jewish Holidays: A Brief Introduction for Christians *By Rabbi Kerry M. Olitzky and Rabbi Daniel Judson* 5½ x 8½, 176 pp, Quality PB, 978-1-58023-302-6 **$16.99***

Jewish Ritual: A Brief Introduction for Christians
By Rabbi Kerry M. Olitzky and Rabbi Daniel Judson 5½ x 8½, 144 pp, Quality PB, 978-1-58023-210-4 **$14.99***

Jewish Spirituality: A Brief Introduction for Christians *By Rabbi Lawrence Kushner*
5½ x 8½, 112 pp, Quality PB, 978-1-58023-150-3 **$12.95***

* A book from Jewish Lights, SkyLight Paths' sister imprint

Spirituality / Animal Companions

Blessing the Animals
Prayers and Ceremonies to Celebrate God's Creatures, Wild and Tame
Edited and with Introductions by Lynn L. Caruso
5 x 7¼, 256 pp, Quality PB, 978-1-59473-253-9 **$15.99**; HC, 978-1-59473-145-7 **$19.99**

Remembering My Pet
A Kid's Own Spiritual Workbook for When a Pet Dies
By Nechama Liss-Levinson, PhD, and Rev. Molly Phinney Baskette, MDiv
Foreword by Lynn L. Caruso
8 x 10, 48 pp, 2-color text, HC, 978-1-59473-221-8 **$16.99**

What Animals Can Teach Us about Spirituality
Inspiring Lessons from Wild and Tame Creatures
By Diana L. Guerrero 6 x 9, 176 pp, Quality PB, 978-1-893361-84-3 **$16.95**

Spirituality & Crafts

Beading—The Creative Spirit
Finding Your Sacred Center through the Art of Beadwork
By Rev. Wendy Ellsworth
Invites you on a spiritual pilgrimage into the kaleidoscope world of glass and color.
7 x 9, 240 pp, 8-page color insert, 40+ b/w photos and 40 diagrams, Quality PB, 978-1-59473-267-6 **$18.99**

Contemplative Crochet
A Hands-On Guide for Interlocking Faith and Craft
By Cindy Crandall-Frazier; Foreword by Linda Skolnik
Illuminates the spiritual lessons you can learn through crocheting.
7 x 9, 208 pp, b/w photos, Quality PB, 978-1-59473-238-6 **$16.99**

The Knitting Way
A Guide to Spiritual Self-Discovery
By Linda Skolnik and Janice MacDaniels
Examines how you can explore and strengthen your spiritual life through knitting.
7 x 9, 240 pp, b/w photos, Quality PB, 978-1-59473-079-5 **$16.99**

The Painting Path
Embodying Spiritual Discovery through Yoga, Brush and Color
By Linda Novick; Foreword by Richard Segalman
Explores the divine connection you can experience through art.
7 x 9, 208 pp, 8-page color insert, plus b/w photos, Quality PB, 978-1-59473-226-3 **$18.99**

The Quilting Path
A Guide to Spiritual Discovery through Fabric, Thread and Kabbalah
By Louise Silk
Explores how to cultivate personal growth through quilt making.
7 x 9, 192 pp, b/w photos and illus., Quality PB, 978-1-59473-206-5 **$16.99**

The Scrapbooking Journey
A Hands-On Guide to Spiritual Discovery
By Cory Richardson-Lauve; Foreword by Stacy Julian
Reveals how this craft can become a practice used to deepen and shape your life.
7 x 9, 176 pp, 8-page color insert, plus b/w photos, Quality PB, 978-1-59473-216-4 **$18.99**

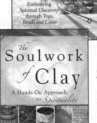

The Soulwork of Clay
A Hands-On Approach to Spirituality
By Marjory Zoet Bankson; Photos by Peter Bankson
Takes you through the seven-step process of making clay into a pot, drawing parallels at each stage to the process of spiritual growth.
7 x 9, 192 pp, b/w photos, Quality PB, 978-1-59473-249-2 **$16.99**

Spiritual Practice—The Sacred Art of Living Series

Dreaming—The Sacred Art: Incubating, Navigating & Interpreting
Sacred Dreams for Spiritual & Personal Growth
By Lori Joan Swick
This fascinating introduction to sacred dreams celebrates the dream experience
as a way to deepen spiritual awareness and as a source of self-healing. Designed
for the novice and the experienced sacred dreamer of all faith traditions, or none.
5½ x 8½, 224 pp, Quality PB, 978-1-59473-544-8 **$16.99**

Conversation—The Sacred Art: Practicing Presence in an Age of Distraction
By Diane M. Millis, PhD; Foreword by Rev. Tilden Edwards, PhD
5½ x 8½, 192 pp, Quality PB, 978-1-59473-474-8 **$16.99**

Dance—The Sacred Art: The Joy of Movement as a Spiritual Practice
By Cynthia Winton-Henry 5½ x 8½, 224 pp, Quality PB, 978-1-59473-268-3 **$16.99**

Fly-Fishing—The Sacred Art: Casting a Fly as a Spiritual Practice
*By Rabbi Eric Eisenkramer and Rev. Michael Attas, MD; Foreword by Chris Wood, CEO,
Trout Unlimited; Preface by Lori Simon, executive director, Casting for Recovery*
5½ x 8½, 160 pp, Quality PB, 978-1-59473-299-7 **$16.99**

Giving—The Sacred Art: Creating a Lifestyle of Generosity
By Lauren Tyler Wright 5½ x 8½, 208 pp, Quality PB, 978-1-59473-224-9 **$16.99**

Haiku—The Sacred Art: A Spiritual Practice in Three Lines
By Margaret D. McGee 5½ x 8½, 192 pp, Quality PB, 978-1-59473-269-0 **$16.99**

Hospitality—The Sacred Art: Discovering the Hidden Spiritual Power of Invitation
and Welcome *By Rev. Nanette Sawyer; Foreword by Rev. Dirk Ficca*
5½ x 8½, 208 pp, Quality PB, 978-1-59473-228-7 **$16.99**

Labyrinths from the Outside In, 2nd Edition: Walking to Spiritual Insight—A
Beginner's Guide *By Rev. Dr. Donna Schaper and Rev. Dr. Carole Ann Camp*
6 x 9, 208 pp, b/w illus. and photos, Quality PB, 978-1-59473-486-1 **$16.99**

Lectio Divina—**The Sacred Art**
Transforming Words & Images into Heart-Centered Prayer
By Christine Valters Paintner, PhD 5½ x 8½, 240 pp, Quality PB, 978-1-59473-300-0 **$16.99**

Pilgrimage—The Sacred Art: Journey to the Center of the Heart
By Dr. Sheryl A. Kujawa-Holbrook 5½ x 8½, 240 pp, Quality PB, 978-1-59473-472-4 **$16.99**

Practicing the Sacred Art of Listening: A Guide to Enrich Your Relationships
and Kindle Your Spiritual Life *By Kay Lindahl* 8 x 8, 176 pp, Quality PB, 978-1-893361-85-0 **$18.99**

Recovery—The Sacred Art: The Twelve Steps as Spiritual Practice *by Rami Shapiro;
Foreword by Joan Borysenko, PhD* 5½ x 8½, 240 pp, Quality PB, 978-1-59473-259-1 **$16.99**

Running—The Sacred Art: Preparing to Practice *By Dr. Warren A. Kay; Foreword by
Kristin Armstrong* 5½ x 8½, 160 pp, Quality PB, 978-1-59473-227-0 **$16.99**

The Sacred Art of Chant: Preparing to Practice
By Ana Hernández 5½ x 8½, 192 pp, Quality PB, 978-1-59473-036-8 **$16.99**

The Sacred Art of Fasting: Preparing to Practice
By Thomas Ryan, CSP 5½ x 8½, 192 pp, Quality PB, 978-1-59473-078-8 **$15.99**

The Sacred Art of Forgiveness: Forgiving Ourselves and Others through God's Grace
By Marcia Ford 8 x 8, 176 pp, Quality PB, 978-1-59473-175-4 **$18.99**

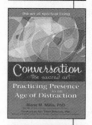

The Sacred Art of Listening: Forty Reflections for Cultivating a Spiritual Practice
By Kay Lindahl; Illus. by Amy Schnapper 8 x 8, 160 pp, b/w illus., Quality PB, 978-1-893361-44-7 **$16.99**

The Sacred Art of Lovingkindness: Preparing to Practice
By Rabbi Rami Shapiro; Foreword by Marcia Ford 5½ x 8½, 176 pp, Quality PB, 978-1-59473-151-8 **$16.99**

Thanking & Blessing—The Sacred Art: Spiritual Vitality through Gratefulness
By Jay Marshall, PhD; Foreword by Philip Gulley 5½ x 8½, 176 pp, Quality PB, 978-1-59473-231-7 **$16.99**

Writing—The Sacred Art: Beyond the Page to Spiritual Practice
By Rami Shapiro and Aaron Shapiro 5½ x 8½, 192 pp, Quality PB, 978-1-59473-372-7 **$16.99**

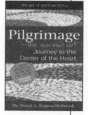

From Jewish Lights, SkyLight Paths' sister imprint
Inspiration

Saying No and Letting Go: Jewish Wisdom on Making Room for What Matters Most
By Rabbi Edwin Goldberg, DHL; Foreword by Rabbi Naomi Levy
Taps into timeless Jewish wisdom that teaches how to "hold on tightly" to the things that matter most while learning to "let go lightly" of the demands and worries that do not ultimately matter. 6 x 9, 192 pp, Quality PB, 978-1-58023-670-6 **$16.99**

The Bridge to Forgiveness: Stories and Prayers for Finding God and Restoring Wholeness By Rabbi Karyn D. Kedar 6 x 9, 176 pp, Quality PB, 978-1-58023-451-1 **$16.99**

The Empty Chair: Finding Hope and Joy—Timeless Wisdom from a Hasidic Master, Rebbe Nachman of Breslov Adapted by Moshe Mykoff and the Breslov Research Institute
4 x 6, 128 pp, Deluxe PB w/ flaps, 978-1-879045-67-5 **$9.99**

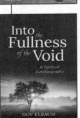

A Formula for Proper Living: Practical Lessons from Life and Torah
By Rabbi Abraham J. Twerski, MD 6 x 9, 144 pp, HC, 978-1-58023-402-3 **$19.99**

The Gentle Weapon: Prayers for Everyday and Not-So-Everyday Moments—Timeless Wisdom from the Teachings of the Hasidic Master, Rebbe Nachman of Breslov
Adapted by Moshe Mykoff and S. C. Mizrahi, together with the Breslov Research Institute
4 x 6, 144 pp, Deluxe PB w/ flaps, 978-1-58023-022-3 **$9.99**

The God Upgrade: Finding Your 21st-Century Spirituality in Judaism's 5,000-Year-Old Tradition By Rabbi Jamie Korngold; Foreword by Rabbi Harold M. Schulweis
6 x 9, 176 pp, Quality PB, 978-1-58023-443-6 **$15.99**

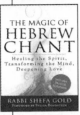

God Whispers: Stories of the Soul, Lessons of the Heart By Rabbi Karyn D. Kedar
6 x 9, 176 pp, Quality PB, 978-1-58023-088-9 **$16.99**

God's To-Do List: 103 Ways to Be an Angel and Do God's Work on Earth
By Dr. Ron Wolfson 6 x 9, 144 pp, Quality PB, 978-1-58023-301-9 **$16.99**

Happiness and the Human Spirit: The Spirituality of Becoming the Best You Can Be
By Rabbi Abraham J. Twerski, MD
6 x 9, 176 pp, Quality PB, 978-1-58023-404-7 **$16.99**; HC, 978-1-58023-343-9 **$19.99**

Into the Fullness of the Void: A Spiritual Autobiography By Dov Elbaum
6 x 9, 304 pp, Quality PB Original, 978-1-58023-715-4 **$18.99**

Life's Daily Blessings: Inspiring Reflections on Gratitude and Joy for Every Day, Based on Jewish Wisdom By Rabbi Kerry M. Olitzky 4½ x 6½, 368 pp, Quality PB, 978-1-58023-396-5 **$16.99**

The Magic of Hebrew Chant: Healing the Spirit, Transforming the Mind, Deepening Love By Rabbi Shefa Gold; Foreword by Sylvia Boorstein
6 x 9, 352 pp, Quality PB, 978-1-58023-671-3 **$24.99**

Restful Reflections: Nighttime Inspiration to Calm the Soul, Based on Jewish Wisdom
By Rabbi Kerry M. Olitzky and Rabbi Lori Forman-Jacobi 4½ x 6½, 448 pp, Quality PB, 978-1-58023-091-9 **$16.99**

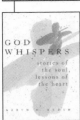

Sacred Intentions: Morning Inspiration to Strengthen the Spirit, Based on Jewish Wisdom
By Rabbi Kerry M. Olitzky and Rabbi Lori Forman-Jacobi 4½ x 6½, 448 pp, Quality PB, 978-1-58023-061-2 **$16.99**

The Seven Questions You're Asked in Heaven: Reviewing and Renewing Your Life on Earth By Dr. Ron Wolfson 6 x 9, 176 pp, Quality PB, 978-1-58023-407-8 **$16.99**

Kabbalah / Mysticism

Ehyeh: A Kabbalah for Tomorrow
By Rabbi Arthur Green, PhD 6 x 9, 224 pp, Quality PB, 978-1-58023-213-5 **$18.99**

The Gift of Kabbalah: Discovering the Secrets of Heaven, Renewing Your Life on Earth
By Tamar Frankiel, PhD 6 x 9, 256 pp, Quality PB, 978-1-58023-141-1 **$16.95**

Jewish Mysticism and the Spiritual Life: Classical Texts, Contemporary Reflections Edited by Dr. Lawrence Fine, Dr. Eitan Fishbane and Rabbi Or N. Rose
6 x 9, 256 pp, HC, 978-1-58023-434-4 **$24.99**; Quality PB, 978-1-58023-719-2 **$18.99**

Seek My Face: A Jewish Mystical Theology By Rabbi Arthur Green, PhD
6 x 9, 304 pp, Quality PB, 978-1-58023-130-5 **$19.95**

Zohar: Annotated & Explained Translation & Annotation by Dr. Daniel C. Matt; Foreword by Andrew Harvey 5½ x 8½, 176 pp, Quality PB, 978-1-893361-51-5 **$16.99**

Personal Growth

Decision Making & Spiritual Discernment
The Sacred Art of Finding Your Way
By Nancy L. Bieber
Presents three essential aspects of Spirit-led decision making: willingness, attentiveness and responsiveness.
5½ x 8½, 208 pp, Quality PB, 978-1-59473-289-8 **$16.99**

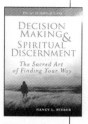

Like a Child
Restoring the Awe, Wonder, Joy and Resiliency of the Human Spirit
By Rev. Timothy J. Mooney
By breaking free from our misperceptions about what it means to be an adult, we can reshape our world and become harbingers of grace. This unique spiritual resource explores Jesus's counsel to become like children in order to enter the kingdom of God.
6 x 9, 160 pp, Quality PB, 978-1-59473-543-1 **$16.99**

Secrets of a Soulful Marriage
Creating & Sustaining a Loving, Sacred Relationship
By Jim Sharon, EdD, and Ruth Sharon, MS
An innovative, hope-filled resource for developing soulful, mature love for committed couples who are looking to create, maintain and glorify the sacred in their relationship. Offers a banquet of practical tools, inspirational real-life stories and spiritual practices for couples of all faiths, or none.
6 x 9, 200 pp (est), Quality PB, 978-1-59473-554-7 **$16.99**

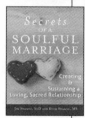

Conversation—The Sacred Art
Practicing Presence in an Age of Distraction
By Diane M. Millis, PhD; Foreword by Rev. Tilden Edwards, PhD
Cultivate the potential for deeper connection in every conversation.
5½ x 8½, 192 pp, Quality PB, 978-1-59473-474-8 **$16.99**

Hospitality—The Sacred Art
Discovering the Hidden Spiritual Power of Invitation and Welcome
By Rev. Nanette Sawyer; Foreword by Rev. Dirk Ficca
Discover how the qualities of hospitality can deepen your self-understanding and help you build transforming and lasting relationships with others and with God.
5½ x 8½, 208 pp, Quality PB, 978-1-59473-228-7 **$16.99**

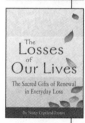

The Losses of Our Lives
The Sacred Gifts of Renewal in Everyday Loss
By Dr. Nancy Copeland-Payton
Shows us that by becoming aware of what our lesser losses have to teach us, the larger losses become less terrifying. Includes spiritual practices and questions for reflection.
6 x 9, 192 pp, Quality PB, 978-1-59473-307-9 **$16.99**; HC, 978-1-59473-271-3 **$19.99**

A Spirituality for Brokenness
Discovering Your Deepest Self in Difficult Times
By Terry Taylor
Compassionately guides you through the practicalities of facing and finally accepting brokenness in your life—a process that can ultimately bring mending.
6 x 9, 176 pp, Quality PB, 978-1-59473-229-4 **$16.99**

The Bridge to Forgiveness
Stories and Prayers for Finding God and Restoring Wholeness
By Karyn D. Kedar
This inspiring guide for healing and wholeness supplies you with a map to help you along your forgiveness journey. Deeply personal stories, comforting prayers and intimate meditations gently lead you through the steps that allow the heart to forgive.
6 x 9, 176 pp, Quality PB, 978-1-58023-451-1 **$16.99***

* A book from Jewish Lights, SkyLight Paths' sister imprint

Retirement and Later-Life Spirituality

Caresharing
A Reciprocal Approach to Caregiving and Care Receiving in the Complexities of Aging, Illness or Disability
By Marty Richards
Shows how to move from independent to *inter*dependent caregiving, so that the "cared for" and the "carer" share a deep sense of connection.
6 x 9, 256 pp, Quality PB, 978-1-59473-286-7 **$16.99**; HC, 978-1-59473-247-8 **$24.99**

How Did I Get to Be 70 When I'm 35 Inside?
Spiritual Surprises of Later Life
By Linda Douty
Encourages you to focus on the inner changes of aging to help you greet your later years as the grand adventure they can be.
6 x 9, 208 pp, Quality PB, 978-1-59473-297-3 **$16.99**

Soul Fire
Accessing Your Creativity
By Thomas Ryan, CSP
This inspiring guide shows you how to cultivate your creative spirit, particularly in the second half of life, as a way to encourage personal growth, enrich your spiritual life and deepen your communion with God.
6 x 9, 160 pp, Quality PB, 978-1-59473-243-0 **$16.99**

Restoring Life's Missing Pieces
The Spiritual Power of Remembering & Reuniting with People, Places, Things & Self
By Caren Goldman; Foreword by Dr. Nancy Copeland-Payton
Delve deeply into ways that your body, mind and spirit answer the Spirit of Re-union's calls to reconnect with people, places, things and self. A powerful and thought-provoking look at "reunions" of all kinds as roads to remembering the missing pieces of our stories, psyches and souls.
6 x 9, 208 pp, Quality PB, 978-1-59473-295-9 **$16.99**

Creative Aging
Rethinking Retirement and Non-Retirement in a Changing World
By Marjory Zoet Bankson
Explores the spiritual dimensions of retirement and aging and offers creative ways for you to share your gifts and experience, particularly when retirement leaves you questioning who you are when you are no longer defined by your career.
6 x 9, 160 pp, Quality PB, 978-1-59473-281-2 **$16.99**

Creating a Spiritual Retirement
A Guide to the Unseen Possibilities in Our Lives
By Molly Srode
Retirement can be an opportunity to refocus on your soul and deepen the presence of spirit in your life. With fresh spiritual reflections and questions to help you explore this new phase.
6 x 9, 208 pp, b/w photos, Quality PB, 978-1-59473-050-4 **$14.99**

Keeping Spiritual Balance as We Grow Older
More than 65 Creative Ways to Use Purpose, Prayer, and the Power of Spirit to Build a Meaningful Retirement
By Molly and Bernie Srode
As we face new demands on our bodies, it's easy to focus on the physical and forget about the transformations in our spiritual selves. This book is brimming with creative, practical ideas to add purpose and spirit to a meaningful retirement.
8 x 8, 224 pp, Quality PB, 978-1-59473-042-9 **$16.99**

Women's Interest

Birthing God: Women's Experiences of the Divine
By Lana Dalberg; Foreword by Kathe Schaaf
Powerful narratives of suffering, love and hope that inspire both personal and collective transformation. 6 x 9, 304 pp, Quality PB, 978-1-59473-480-9 **$18.99**

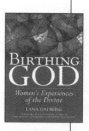

On the Chocolate Trail: A Delicious Adventure Connecting Jews, Religions, History, Travel, Rituals and Recipes to the Magic of Cacao
By Rabbi Deborah R. Prinz
Take a delectable journey through the religious history of chocolate—a real treat!
6 x 9, 272 pp, 20+ b/w photographs, Quality PB, 978-1-58023-487-0 **$18.99***

Women, Spirituality and Transformative Leadership
Where Grace Meets Power
Edited by Kathe Schaaf, Kay Lindahl, Kathleen S. Hurty, PhD, and Reverend Guo Cheen
A dynamic conversation on the power of women's spiritual leadership and its emerging patterns of transformation.
6 x 9, 288 pp, Quality PB, 978-1-59473-548-6 **$18.99**; HC, 978-1-59473-313-0 **$24.99**

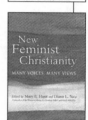

Spiritually Healthy Divorce: Navigating Disruption with Insight & Hope
By Carolyne Call A spiritual map to help you move through the twists and turns of divorce. 6 x 9, 224 pp, Quality PB, 978-1-59473-288-1 **$16.99**

New Feminist Christianity: Many Voices, Many Views
Edited by Mary E. Hunt and Diann L. Neu
Insights from ministers and theologians, activists and leaders, artists and liturgists offer a starting point for building new models of religious life and worship.
6 x 9, 384 pp, Quality PB, 978-1-59473-435-9 **$19.99**; HC, 978-1-59473-285-0 **$24.99**

Bread, Body, Spirit: Finding the Sacred in Food
Edited and with Introductions by Alice Peck 6 x 9, 224 pp, Quality PB, 978-1-59473-242-3 **$19.99**

Dance—The Sacred Art: The Joy of Movement as a Spiritual Practice
By Cynthia Winton-Henry 5½ x 8½, 224 pp, Quality PB, 978-1-59473-268-3 **$16.99**

Daughters of the Desert: Stories of Remarkable Women from Christian, Jewish and Muslim Traditions
By Claire Rudolf Murphy, Meghan Nuttall Sayres, Mary Cronk Farrell, Sarah Conover and Betsy Wharton
5½ x 8½, 192 pp, Illus., Quality PB, 978-1-59473-106-8 **$14.99** Inc. reader's discussion guide

The Divine Feminine in Biblical Wisdom Literature
Selections Annotated & Explained
Translation & Annotation by Rabbi Rami Shapiro; Foreword by Rev. Cynthia Bourgeault, PhD
5½ x 8½, 240 pp, Quality PB, 978-1-59473-109-9 **$16.99**

Divining the Body: Reclaim the Holiness of Your Physical Self
By Jan Phillips 8 x 8, 256 pp, Quality PB, 978-1-59473-080-1 **$18.99**

Honoring Motherhood: Prayers, Ceremonies & Blessings
Edited and with Introductions by Lynn L. Caruso
5 x 7¼, 272 pp, Quality PB, 978-1-58473-384-0 **$9.99**; HC, 978-1-59473-239-3 **$19.99**

Next to Godliness: Finding the Sacred in Housekeeping
Edited by Alice Peck 6 x 9, 224 pp, Quality PB, 978-1-59473-214-0 **$19.99**

ReVisions: Seeing Torah through a Feminist Lens
By Rabbi Elyse Goldstein 5½ x 8½, 224 pp, Quality PB, 978-1-58023-117-6 **$16.95***

The Triumph of Eve & Other Subversive Bible Tales
By Matt Biers-Ariel 5½ x 8½, 192 pp, Quality PB, 978-1-59473-176-1 **$14.99**

White Fire: A Portrait of Women Spiritual Leaders in America
By Malka Drucker; Photos by Gay Block 7 x 10, 320 pp, b/w photos, HC, 978-1-893361-64-5 **$24.95**

Woman Spirit Awakening in Nature: Growing Into the Fullness of Who You Are
By Nancy Barrett Chickerneo, PhD; Foreword by Eileen Fisher
8 x 8, 224 pp, b/w illus., Quality PB, 978-1-59473-250-8 **$16.99**

Women of Color Pray: Voices of Strength, Faith, Healing, Hope and Courage
Edited and with Introductions by Christal M. Jackson
5 x 7¼, 208 pp, Quality PB, 978-1-59473-077-1 **$15.99**

* A book from Jewish Lights, SkyLight Paths' sister imprint

About SKYLIGHT PATHS Publishing

SkyLight Paths Publishing is creating a place where people of different spiritual traditions come together for challenge and inspiration, a place where we can help each other understand the mystery that lies at the heart of our existence.

Through spirituality, our religious beliefs are increasingly becoming a part of our lives—rather than *apart* from our lives. While many of us may be more interested than ever in spiritual growth, we may be less firmly planted in traditional religion. Yet, we do want to deepen our relationship to the sacred, to learn from our own as well as from other faith traditions, and to practice in new ways.

SkyLight Paths sees both believers and seekers as a community that increasingly transcends traditional boundaries of religion and denomination—people wanting to learn from each other, *walking together, finding the way*.

For your information and convenience, at the back of this book we have provided a list of other SkyLight Paths books you might find interesting and useful. They cover the following subjects:

Buddhism / Zen	Gnosticism	Poetry
Catholicism	Hinduism / Vedanta	Prayer
Chaplaincy		Religious Etiquette
Children's Books	Inspiration	Retirement & Later-
Christianity	Islam / Sufism	Life Spirituality
Comparative Religion	Judaism	Spiritual Biography
	Meditation	Spiritual Direction
Earth-Based Spirituality	Mindfulness	Spirituality
	Monasticism	Women's Interest
Enneagram	Mysticism	Worship
Global Spiritual Perspectives	Personal Growth	

Or phone, fax, mail or email to: SKYLIGHT PATHS Publishing
Sunset Farm Offices, Route 4 • P.O. Box 237 • Woodstock, Vermont 05091
Tel: (802) 457-4000 • Fax: (802) 457-4004 • www.skylightpaths.com
Credit card orders: (800) 962-4544 (8:30AM–5:30PM EST Monday–Friday)
Generous discounts on quantity orders. SATISFACTION GUARANTEED. Prices subject to change.